Tecpán Guatemala

Westview Case Studies in Anthropology

Series Editor: EDWARD F. FISCHER
Vanderbilt University

Tecpán Guatemala: A Modern Maya Town in Global and Local Context, Edward F. Fischer (Vanderbilt University) and Carol Hendrickson (Marlboro College)

Daughters of Tunis: Women, Family, and Networks in a Muslim City, Paula Holmes-Eber (University of Washington)

Fulbe Voices: Marriage, Islam, and Medicine in Northern Cameroon, Helen A. Regis (Louisiana State University)

Forthcoming:

The Lao: Gender, Power, and Livelihood, Carol Ireson-Doolittle (Willamette University) and Geraldine Moreno-Black (University of Oregon)

Tecpán Guatemala

*A Modern Maya Town in Global
and Local Context*

EDWARD F. FISCHER
Vanderbilt University
CAROL HENDRICKSON
Marlboro College

A Member of the Perseus Books Group

Copyright © 2003 by Westview Press, A Member of the Perseus Books Group.

A Cataloguing-in-Publication data record for this book is available from the Library of Congress.
ISBN 0-8133-4034-9 (HC)
ISBN-10: 0-8133-3722-4   ISBN-13: 978-0-8133-3722-7 (Pbk.)

All photographs taken by authors unless otherwise noted.

Westview Press books are available at special discounts for bulk purchases in the United States by corporations, institutions, and other organizations. For more information, please contact the Special Markets Department at the Perseus Books Group, 11 Cambridge Center, Cambridge, MA 02142, or call (617) 252-5298.

Published in 2002 in the United States of America by Westview Press, 5500 Central Avenue, Boulder, Colorado 80301-2877, and in the United Kingdom by Westview Press, 12 Hid's Copse Road, Cumnor Hill, Oxford OX2 9JJ.

Find us on the World Wide Web at www.westviewpress.com
The paper used in this publication meets the requirements of the American National Standard for Permanence of Paper for Printed Library Materials Z39.48–1984.

Contents

Series Editor Preface

We are constantly reminded by media pundits, academics, and business leaders that the world is a much smaller place than it once was. As proof, we simply have to look around us: overnight delivery and e-mail have accelerated the pace and expanded the possibilities of social and commercial interaction; the Internet has spawned long-distance friendships and collaborations that seamlessly span continents and time zones; much of our clothing and other consumer goods are assembled abroad. We have a good idea of what all of this means to us, but what does it mean to them, those who live at the periphery of the globalized economy? And what can we learn from anthropology about this rapidly changing world?

To address these questions this book looks at the case of Tecpán, a predominantly Maya town in the Guatemalan highlands. Carol Hendrickson and I examine the historical *longue durée* as well as contemporary economic and political contexts in which Tecpanecos constantly and creatively remake their lives. Our goal is to present Tecpanecos not as exotic Others but as individuals living their lives under very different (although interrelated) social and material circumstances from our own. We look at change as well as continuity—not just how Tecpanecos react and adapt to circumstances imposed from afar, but how they assert their own culturally informed interests. We document the workings of *cofradías* and traditional Maya religious ceremonies as well as the arrival of an Internet café in town and a switch from growing corn to producing export crops for the global market. In short, we try to convey the vast complexity of life in this small town, the contradictions as well as consistencies of being Maya in the modern world. We juxtapose elements of the modern with the traditional in our descriptions (a strategy visually captured in the cover photograph). In a way, this plays to our own postmodern attraction to such seeming ironies, but we must keep in mind that the irony is ours, not theirs: The Tecpanecos we describe are earnestly living their lives, doing the best they can under trying circumstances.

Ethnographic fieldwork is a dialectic process. Anthropologists build analytic models based on observed behavior and informant explications. These are constantly constructed and then just as quickly broken down by the endless diversity of observed experience. As anthropologists, we attempt to make sense of the world we observe, but this is not, as was once thought, a matter of mastering a finite set of data and working out rules of interrelationships. "Culture" is more a process or a space of interaction than a thing or a static body of knowledge. And so, even as we try to figure out the workings of the world around us, the very rules of the game are subtly changing. As good as our tools of analysis may be, we are always one step behind contemporary events. One never masters "the field" in ethnography.

What we present here is an incomplete and biased look at Tecpán culture, coming from our unique experiences working there over a twenty-year period. We focus on Kaqchikel Tecpanecos, devoting little space to the lives of non-Indian (or *ladino*) residents. This presents a biased perspective, but accurately reflects our interests and the strengths of our data. It also reveals our self-positioning in the politicized context of Guatemala's inter-ethnic relations. Although sympathetic to the plight of *ladino* Guatemalans, we feel that our primary obligation is to the Maya people, and especially those individuals who have so selflessly opened their lives to us. Our greatest desire is for our work, in some small way, to benefit the people we study by increasing awareness of their situation.

Tecpán Guatemala is the first volume in the new Westview Case Studies in Anthropology series. This book, along with the other volumes in the series, seeks to build on the traditional strengths of ethnography while rejecting overly romantic and isolationist tendencies in the genre. This series brings the short ethnography format up to date in terms of data, theory, and representational style while retaining the unique and invaluable perspective built up from the observed complexity of on-the-ground experience.

Anthropology, like other disciplines, has become increasingly specialized over the last decades. As a result, monographs are reaching ever-decreasing audiences. The works in this series resist this trend by making important contributions to ethnographic description and social theory available in a format that will appeal not only to other specialists but to educated audiences in general.

The individuals, communities, and cultures examined in these case studies are portrayed not as the exotic isolates of an earlier era but as active agents enmeshed in global as well as local systems of politics, economics, and cultural flows. There is a focus on contemporary ways of life, forces of social change, and creative responses to novel situations as well as the more traditional concerns of classic ethnographies. In presenting rich humanistic and social scientific data born of the dialectic engagement of fieldwork, the books in this series move toward realizing the full pedagogical potential of anthropology, imparting to the reader an empathetic understanding of alternative ways of viewing and acting in the world as well as a solid basis for critical thought regarding the historically contingent nature of cultural boundaries and knowledge.

EDWARD F. FISCHER
Vanderbilt University

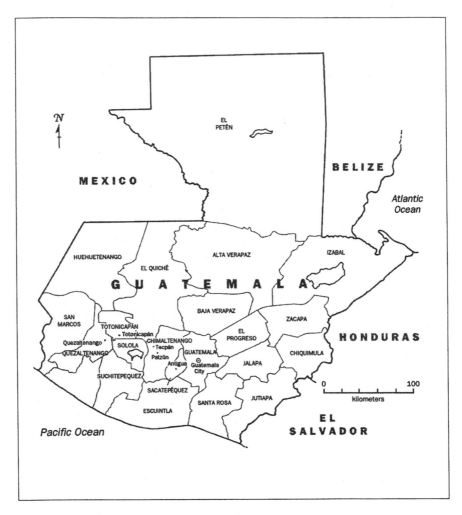

Guatemala, with Tecpán and department names noted.

Introduction

This book is about the indigenous people of Tecpán Guatemala, a predominantly Kaqchikel Maya town in the Guatemalan highlands. It is concerned with the rhythms and rituals of everyday life—what an outsider might find "foreign" but which a Tecpaneco (or person from Tecpán) would probably find familiar, as well as what they consider new, problematic, and challenging. Using fieldwork and historical data analyzed through the lenses of contemporary theoretical frames, we hope to paint a portrait of Tecpán that conveys the complexity of social life and of individual actions. At the same time we consciously resist the temptation to portray it as an isolated community, removed from the global forces that affect our own lives. Rather we describe Tecpán as an integrated part of larger arenas of activity: the Kaqchikel region, the central highlands, the Guatemalan state, and global systems.

For outsiders (foreigners as well as non-Maya Guatemalans), the Maya are most often thought of as the creators of a grand pre-Columbian civilization marked by large city-states, hieroglyphic writing, and impressive scientific advances. But Maya peoples and Maya cultures persevere, some 8 million living in what is today southern Mexico, Belize, Honduras, and Guatemala. In Guatemala, Maya Indians make up about half of the total population, one of the highest concentrations of native peoples in the hemisphere. Maya culture has changed dramatically over the centuries, with the devastating effects of Spanish contact, diseases, and colonialism having etched an indelible impression on Maya lifeways. Yet, at the same time, the Maya have demonstrated a sustained cultural resilience, adapting to new contingencies while retaining certain beliefs and behaviors with deep historical roots.

It is fashionable in anthropology at the turn of the twenty-first century to dismiss attempts to document autochthonous cultural traits, the truly indigenous (and thus authentic) customs that have survived the passage of time. As critics rightly point out, culture is an ongoing hybrid construction built by individuals caught up in the immediacies of everyday life; the hunt for cultural "survivals" romanticizes this process and negates the very real intentions of cultural actors, reducing them to trait lists. At the same time, history and tradition do play an important role in the construction of culture. Working among Kaqchikel Maya people in Tecpán, probably the most common response to our meddlesome anthropological questions about why things are done a certain way or why particular acts are performed was simply that "it is our custom," a sometimes aggravating response for the fieldworker yearning for detailed explanations, but revealing all the same. Doing things for tradition's sake alone is a salient motivating factor for many Kaqchikel Tecpanecos. This is not to imply that modern Maya peoples are somehow slaves to tradition in a way in which we ourselves are not. The Maya are arguably much more culturally conservative in certain aspects of their life, but in many ways they are just as engaged in global systems of politics, economics, and cultural identities as the foreigners who come to live in their communities.

WRITING THIS BOOK

Co-authoring an ethnographic monograph such as this provides a unique opportunity to present multiple perspectives on the same events and phenomena, all the better in this case as the authors have different perspectives based on gender, the moments in history when they lived in Tecpán, and the questions they investigated. While trying to avoid self-indulgent autobiography but mindful of the need for reflexive insights, we have inserted ourselves into the narrative of this book to distinguish our unique field experiences and points of view. When we do this we refer to ourselves in the third person using our first names, Carol and Ted.

Ted first visited Tecpán in the summer of 1990 while a student in Tulane University's Kaqchikel Language and Culture School. During that summer Ted met Carol and a number of people from Tecpán and decided to study the vibrant local market for his dissertation research. He returned in the summer of 1991, rented a sparse room in the Hotel Iximché, and mapped out the Thursday market and talked to local vendors. It was an especially auspicious summer for Ted, for it was at a Maya ceremony in a hamlet of Tecpán that he met his future wife, Mareike Sattler (a student of epigraphy and linguistics who was in Guatemala learning Kaqchikel). On a return trip in 1992, Ted decided to switch his topic from Tecpán marketing strategies to the dramatic emergence of a pan-Maya movement in Guatemala, a movement in which many of the leaders were from Tecpán. In 1993 and 1994 Ted and Mareike lived and worked in Tecpán, based in a two-room former Mennonite school house; they have returned on several occasions to visit friends and conduct follow-up research.

After graduating from college with a degree in mathematics, Carol decided to learn more about the world and became a 4-H Youth Development Program volunteer working with the Ministry of Agriculture in southeastern Guatemala. During June 1974, while on vacation from her job and studying weaving in the highland town of Comalapa, she visited neighboring Tecpán briefly, completely unaware of what her future relationship with the town would be. Her experiences in Guatemala—and in the highlands in particular—led her to study anthropology in graduate school and to focus her research on the ways *traje* (Maya dress) reflects social identity. By the time she returned to the highlands in 1979, much had changed. A massive earthquake in 1976 had leveled towns in the central highlands—Tecpán was one of those most severely hit—and by the end of the 1970s the Guatemalan civil war was entering its most intense stage. Carol had planned on working in Nebaj, but violence in the area necessitated a change and she decided to work in Tecpán as much for its proximity to the Pan-American Highway and speedy exit from the area as for its active textile tradition. She lived in Tecpán in 1980–1981 and has returned numerous times.

READING THIS BOOK

To give the reader a multifaceted sense of everyday life in Tecpán—particularly the lives of people living in the *cabecera* (town center)—we present a composite portrait of the town, combining perspectives from many different angles. Sections and chapters divide up fragmented aspects of Tecpán experience into manageable topics, but throughout these divisions we interweave observations and analyses, our own personal perspectives, and the thoughts and words of Tecpanecos as well as those of other anthropologists and students of Latin America. In each chapter we have incorporated explicit reference to contemporary theoretical issues in anthropology and the social sciences, but always firmly grounded in the slippery particularities of our ethnographic perspectives on Tecpán. Although we think of the chapters as having a particular flow, readers may choose to read them in another order or to focus on particular sections; we have tried to write each so that there is the possibility of it being read as a free-standing piece.

The first several chapters present basic background information for understanding the contemporary Guatemalan context, with an eye toward Tecpán. Chapter 1 gives a general introduction to Tecpán today, providing the sort of background information that a person visiting the town for the first time in the company of an anthropologist might expect to learn. Chapter 2 looks at Guatemala's recent political history, with a focus on the violence of the late 1970s and early 1980s, to set the larger context in which Tecpanecos live their lives. In Chapter 3 we expand this background context to include a brief history of Maya peoples in general and the Kaqchikeles of the Tecpán region in particular. Chapter 4 begins by describing Tecpán's experiences following a devastating 1976 earthquake and the subsequent civil war; we conclude by looking at Tecpán's links to Maya cultural revitalization efforts in the 1980s and 1990s.

After these introductory snapshots and historical insights, we turn to the ways in which the Kaqchikeles in Tecpán conceptualize their world. In Chapter 5 we look at Kaqchikel conceptions of the self through a discussion of the metaphysical works of the heart and soul, as well as the complex landscape of religions in Tecpán, and how these are played out in daily interactions and individual world-views. In Chapter 6 we examine the interrelations of language, dress, and the ongoing construction of identities in local culture. We turn to the economic bases of Tecpaneco culture in Chapter 7, focusing on traditional agriculture as well as the many ways that Tecpanecos are increasingly integrated into world markets. The conclusion then brings these various themes and perspectives together, offering a critical synthesis of Tecpaneco life in a globalized world.

Acknowledgments

This book is a collaborative effort in many senses. As authors we have collaborated in writing the text, but what we write about has been gleaned from years of collaboration with friends and acquaintances in Tecpán and colleagues in the United States. In particular, we owe the Cojtí Maxia, Guorón Rodríguez, Lux Sacbajá, Patal Ajzac, Rodríguez Guaján, Tecún Cuxil, and Tecún Rucuch families of Tecpán many thanks for their kindnesses large and small over the years. Also in Guatemala, Alberto Esquit, Raxche', Pakal B'alam, Demetrio Cojtí, the members of OKMA (particularly Lolmay and Waykan), and other Maya scholars and activists have given generously of their time and insights. The Centro de Investigaciones Regionales de Mesoamérica (CIRMA) has provided us with logistical support and an intellectually stimulating retreat in Antigua Guatemala. In the United States, Abigail Adams, Mareike Sattler, and Judie Maxwell provided encouragement and feedback at various stages of the project, and their contributions make this a much richer text. Our work would not have been possible without the material support of several organizations. Ted's work was funded by the Inter-American Foundation, the John D. and Catherine T. MacArthur Foundation, the Wenner-Gren Foundation, and Vanderbilt University. Carol received support from the Fulbright-Hays Faculty Research Abroad Program and Marlboro College. Finally, we would like to thank Karl Yambert and the fine staff at Westview Press for their patience and support in seeing this project to fruition.

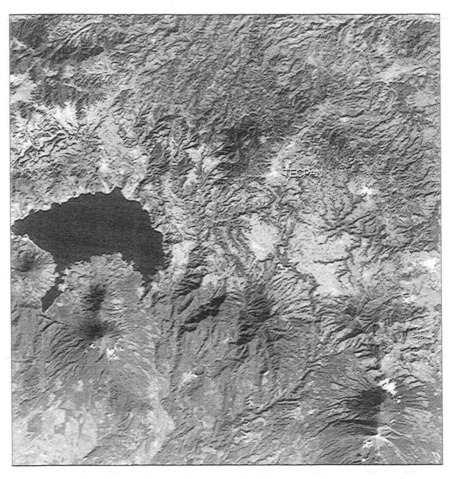

1994 LANDSAT image of highland Guatemala. Note Lake Atitlán on the left, the volcanoes at the bottom separating the highlands from the Pacific Coast plain, and Tecpán in the upper center.

I

Tecpán

A LAND OF CONTRASTS

A place of striking contrasts and deep contradictions, Guatemala eludes easy description. Visitors to this small Central American country (about the size of Tennessee but with an estimated population of just over 12.5 million) are first stuck by the dramatic landscape of the highlands: rich green valleys nestled between imposing mountains, crystalline lakes surrounded by rumbling volcanoes—the evocative clichés of Guatemalan tourist brochures. It does not take long, however, to note the human contrasts as well, as the country is home to both some of the wealthiest and some of the poorest people in Latin America. Shanty towns clinging to ravine slopes ring Guatemala City's affluent neighborhoods, where houses are protected by barbed-wire and glass-shard-topped walls and patrolled by armed guards. Likewise, the peace of the agricultural landscape verdant with crops is punctured by impoverished villages, rutted dirt roads, and bony barking dogs.

Traveling west toward Tecpán from Guatemala City on the Pan-American Highway (the two-lane asphalt road that serves as Guatemala's primary transportation artery), one climbs almost 2,000 feet in little more than 50 kilometers. Ears popping from the rapid change in altitude, travelers are then met by a series of fertile and intensively cultivated valleys, ending in the green expanse of the Tecpán Valley, which is crisscrossed with streams and planted abundantly with corn, beans, and squash as well broccoli, cabbage, and snow peas. On the south side of the Pan-American Highway lies the active volcano chain that divides the highlands from the more temperate Pacific Coastal plain, while on the north rises the older mountain chain of the Continental Divide. In the early 1980s the forested slopes to the west and north of Tecpán's town center were troubled places, home to guerrilla groups,

1

army camps, and refugee settlements as the civil war simmered and exploded. Beyond the forests far to the north, the mountain ranges drop off dramatically, leading into the vast expanse of lowlands covered by dense tropical forest. The hills and mountains closest to town have been largely deforested, accentuating the steep inclines. These are covered in small maize and bean plots or left bare, symbols of such social issues as unequal access to quality agricultural land, the ecological issues of deforestation, and political favoritism in the use of community resources.

One of the two principal entrances to Tecpán lies at kilometer marker 78 on the Pan-American Highway and is marked by a slightly-more-than-human-sized concrete pyramid with text noting that Tecpán was Guatemala's first Spanish capital and the site of the precontact Kaqchikel Maya capital (Iximche'). Jumbled around it and dwarfing this modest monument are billboards with an athletic blond male model hawking Rubios cigarettes; an idealized rendition of a Maya woman handing you a bottle of Quetzalteca Especial grain alcohol; and signature logos of various sodas, electronic products, and local establishments. At almost all hours of the day there are small groups of people standing around on both sides of the highway, waiting for buses to pick them up.

Entering Tecpán, a visitor would have reason to label this a fairly traditional Maya town. The majority (about 70 percent) of its approximately 10,000 residents[1] are indigenous people who speak Kaqchikel Mayan, the native language; most of the women wear the brightly colored, hand-woven dress, and many weave on the backstrap loom. Maya religious life is evident in the centuries-old Catholic church and at shrines and altars around the town, and the large weekly market is a picture book image of the sort of thing tourists flock to the country to see and experience. Tecpán is also a town in flux and firmly ensconced in (if on the periphery of) the global scheme of things. Since the earliest days of Spanish contact, the Kaqchikel Maya of Tecpán have selectively embraced aspects of Spanish—and more broadly Western—life while retaining a clear sense of their own identity. Today, Tecpán is known throughout the region as an affluent and progressive Indian town: trucks and cars increasingly crowd the streets; a bootleg cable system supplies homes with HBO and other foreign fare; an Internet café connects its young customers to the larger world; shopping centers have opened and more are being built; evangelical Protestant churches and those of other Christian religions number in the dozens in town and claim thousands of the faithful; and Tecpán Maya have professional jobs as teachers, bankers, health care providers, and social workers as well as heads of publishing, transportation, and computer operations.

In contrast to the dramatic landscape, the urban setting of Tecpán appears drab, a relic of the hasty reconstruction following the 1976 earthquake. Guidebooks, when they deign to mention it at all, describe Tecpán as an unremarkable place, notable only for its proximity to an archaeological park at Iximche' and the scattering of roadside restaurants along the Pan-American Highway. And so it may seem to the casual visitor, the dusty streets and cinder block buildings not unlike so many other highland Maya towns. There is no souvenir market, nor is it particularly gringo-friendly (some might find the occa-

Figure 1.1   The turnoff to Tecpán from the Pan-American Highway.

sional catcalls and shouts of "gringo" off-putting). Beneath this somewhat gritty veneer, however, lies a place of great interest, both in terms of regional history and modern community organization. Summary guidebook accounts miss the more subtle qualities of life in a place like Tecpán, qualities that reveal themselves only after longer residence.

Over 7,000 feet above sea level, the area is known as *tierra fría* because of the year-round chilly climate. The high altitude has its advantages and disadvantages. Tropical diseases that plague the lowland areas are almost nonexistent. There are few mosquitoes, and certain crops, including a hybrid form of maize, can have multiple harvests every year. But, befitting its geographic designation as *tierra fría*, Tecpán does get cold, . . . a bone-chilling cold especially pronounced during the rainy season, when nothing ever seems to get completely dry. Frosts are common at night around the New Year, and upon waking in the morning one frequently encounters a thin layer of ice around the edges of the *pilas*, the large outdoor sinks that serve as water storage basins. There is nothing quite so invigorating as bathing in the brisk morning air in the icy water of a *pila*. Although the area occasionally reaches freezing temperatures, snow is unheard of, and even on the coldest days the sun shines with an intensity found only at such high altitudes and low latitudes, allowing one to be simultaneously chilled and warmed.

Tecpanecos joke that their town has but two seasons, one muddy and the other dusty. Indeed, the temperature varies only slightly across the seasons, from lows near freezing some nights in late December and early January to daytime highs in the 80s (F) on the occasional sunny July and August day. During *invierno* ("winter" or the rainy season)—when the town's streets turn into impassable

Figure 1.2   The road to Iximche' in 1994 (before it was paved) during the rainy season. Note the procession for San Francisco, the town's patron saint.

rivers—the rain is fairly predictable, coming in heavy showers in the afternoons and/or evenings. In fact, some three-quarters of total yearly rainfall occurs between early May and late October. But this predictability does not make it any less inconvenient: Outside work must be stopped, people are soaked, and clothes often take days to dry. By September everyone is ready to see the end of the rain and mud, if for no other reason than to shake off the lingering chill that accompanies the frigid wetness. But by mid-November almost everything in town is covered by a fine layer of dust, churned up by children playing on packed earth patios and by passing cars and foot traffic on the town's now dusty streets. To protect against the *polvo* (dust) invasion, people are particularly assiduous in covering objects of value in their homes: prime objects for *servilletas* (covering clothes) are TVs, VCRs, radios, blenders, treadle sewing machines, comfy chairs and sofas, computers, and/or cars.

Tecpán is a bi-ethnic town, inhabited by Maya and *ladinos*. Aside from these two groups, there are only occasional transient gringo residents: anthropologists or other foreign students, Peace Corp or other volunteers, and missionaries. There is also one black man living in town, a migrant from the Caribbean coast who plays in a local marimba band. Depending on the context and the person involved, native Tecpanecos refer to themselves, and are referred to by others, as *indígenas*, Maya, *naturales*, Kaqchikeles, or (generally pejoratively) *indios*,[2] and they make up a majority of Tecpán residents (about 70 percent in the town center, and

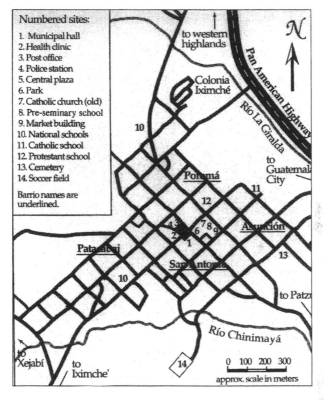

Figure 1.3   Street map of Tecpán.

close to 95 percent in the surrounding countryside). The rest of the population is commonly referred to as *ladinos*, non-Indians of putative Spanish descent. In Kaqchikel, the term *kaxlan* refers to *ladinos* (and more broadly to any non-Maya peoples), and *kaxlan* acts as a modifier in a number of phrases to denote Western-style products: *kaxlan ixim* (*kaxlan* corn or "wheat"), *kaxlan way* (*kaxlan* tortilla or "wheat bread"), and *kaxlan po't* (a Western-style blouse, *po't* referring to the handwoven blouses that Maya women wear). Ethnic tensions between Maya and *ladinos* historically run high in Tecpán (as is true in communities throughout the highlands), a vestige of colonial power relations. At the same time, Tecpanecos often note with pride the genuine harmony and good relations between Indians and *ladinos* that prevail in town today.

OPENING CLOSED COMMUNITIES

Earlier ethnographies of the Maya tended to stress the individuality of communities and their isolated and insulated nature. Eric Wolf (1957) applied the term "closed corporate peasant community" to refer to such social formations that were inward rather than outward looking, resistant to external change, and yet fundamentally unstable. Wolf writes that these communities show "not only a marked tendency to exclude the outsider as a person, but also to limit the flow of outside goods and ideas into the community . . . [they are] socially and culturally isolated from the larger society in which they exist . . . [a position] reinforced by the parochial, localocentric attitudes of the community"(1957: 4–5). At the same time, Wolf situated his model into a formulation of the colonial world system: the closed corporate peasant community was a response to the tributary mode of production imposed by Spaniards and their descendants. Thus he distinguished between "internal functions" (sociocultural isolation) and "external functions" (funneling economic resources), seeing isolation as an internal function that is allowed and reinforced through the mechanisms of tributary extraction, an external function (1957: 11–13).

Wolf published an article in 1986 in which he notes that his early work was "overly schematic and not a little naive" (326). Yet even today there is a tendency to stress the isolation of Maya communities in analyses of Guatemalan society: They speak different languages and dialects, they have lives facing inward to town markets and churches, and Maya from different towns exhibit a seeming unwillingness to join together to fight common problems. Carol Smith (1991) argues that isolation and atomization of rural Maya communities has proven to be an effective strategy for fighting impositions from the Guatemalan state: There are no "one size fits all" policies, and thus many centralized state initiatives are doomed to fail because of the complex of circumstances in the different communities in which they are enacted. Moreover, from precontact times to today, geographic barriers have hindered widespread communication among communities, and community allegiances are certainly strong. Even staunch advocates of pan-Maya activism sometimes exhibit strong town loyalties when interacting with people from other communities.

It is often remarked that the world is a much smaller place today than ever before, and certainly physical mobility and virtual communications have made the world easier to navigate at the turn of the millennium. Anthropologists such as Akhil Gupta and James Ferguson (1992) have argued that this makes models of culture based on particular real world locations dated. But in seemingly marginal global sites such as Tecpán (although here we need to ask, marginal for what people and what purposes?), physical location is still a primary social determinant. Those with whom a person interacts on a daily basis, who have likely known that person since birth, create a social environment in which all must live. These are the hard-to-escape ties of kinship and community.

Yet it is possible to overstate Tecpán's isolation. Tecpanecos and Maya in general have long maintained wide-ranging connections, through both trade and political alliances, dating back to far before the arrival of the Spaniards. During the precontact period, Iximche' had ties with groups as far north as the Aztecs in Central Mexico and likely as far south as Panama. Native documents even record that Montezuma had sent messengers to the Kaqchikel court in 1510 to warn the Kaqchikeles of sightings of strange white peoples in large ships. During the colonial period, the town was linked to regional and national markets, and today Tecpanecos are exceptionally mobile and well traveled by Guatemalan standards. A number of townspeople (mostly young men) have traveled to the United States to study or to work and earn money (part of which is sent home via Western Union, which has a branch in a local bank). More and more households are getting telephones in the aftermath of the national phone company being privatized, and Tecpanecos have proven to be savvy shoppers in the newly competitive market for long distance and international calls. Off the town square there are a number of small video parlors, usually nothing more than a simple store front containing benches, a television, a VCR, and a rental desk. The preferred fare is dubbed kung-fu movies and Rambo-like action films from Hollywood, peppered with an assortment of children's offerings, science fiction, and soft porn from Mexico.

Perhaps the most troubling evidence of global-local ties comes from the violence of the 1980s, a period in which Tecpán, like many other highland Maya communities, found itself in the midst of a complex civil war, fueled by the competing Western ideologies of the Cold War. The violence reached Tecpán in force in 1981. In May of that year, the town priest, a moderately progressive man by most accounts, was shot down outside the parish house on a busy market day. "Unknown men" (the *desconocidos* to whom most such attacks are attributed) drove up on a motorcycle, shot the priest, and roared off. Presumably in retaliation (for the unknown men were almost certainly part of the state's military apparatus), guerrilla troops entered Tecpán's town center in November. The occupation lasted only a few hours, but the individuals involved were able to damage several buildings—the town hall was dynamited and the health center, post office, police headquarters, and jail were riddled with gunfire—and speak with townspeople. It did not take long for the army to arrive in town en masse, and they set up a garrison on the central square that was to remain for eight years. Many people were taken from their homes and to the garrison for questioning, never to return. People were frightened, and fear was palpable in the town. There are no good estimates of how many people were killed or tortured in Tecpán; certainly fewer than in some other towns, although not an insignificant number. There are numerous clandestine graves in the countryside surrounding town. Many people had close relatives killed; all know of someone who suffered the fate. The situation became so dire in 1981 and 1982 that a number of Tecpanecos decided to flee to the safety of the capital or the mountains.

A more mundane example of Tecpán's connectedness to communities beyond its municipal boundaries comes in the form of transportation links, particularly by means of its excellent bus service. A fleet of old Bluebird school buses operating with the red and white colors of the Veloz Poaquileña company runs constantly between Tecpán and Guatemala City between about 4:30 A.M. and 7:00

P.M., leaving from the market building in Tecpán every fifteen or twenty minutes. These are the classic "chicken buses," often filled to overflowing with humans and their baggage, including produce, market goods, and even live chickens. Each of these buses, which are found throughout Guatemala, is slightly different, personalized by its owner with Bible quotes, silhouettes of voluptuous ladies, images of the Virgin Mary and Jesus, hand-painted quotes such as "Díos Nos Guia" ("God Guides Us"), and makeshift radios and cassette decks blaring a mix of static and music. In seats that would normally hold two children, three adults (and their children) are routinely packed like sardines, with those unfortunate enough to be stuck in the aisle forced to sit with their buttocks just barely on the edge of their cushions; other people stand among them in any available space. In addition to the driver, each bus has an *ayudante* who calls out the destination ("a Guate, a Guate, a Guatemalaaaa") and urges on potential customers. With late-comers hanging out the front door and sometimes even latched on to the ladder in back, packed buses may be a comical site for foreign travelers; however, they more often elicit groans from locals who know what it is like to ride like this on a regular basis. The trade-off for such crowded conditions is a low fare; in 1999 it cost 7 quetzals³ (less than $1) for a one-way passage between Tecpán and Guatemala City. Veloz Poaquileño has also added two former tourist buses to their fleet, which, for 8 quetzals, offer individual seats—at least as long as they aren't filled. It takes as long as two and one-half hours to make the trip, with frequent stops along the way to pick up passengers waiting by the side of the road.

Several small bus lines serve Tecpán's satellite *aldeas* (villages), and during the large Thursday market a number of buses travel to the neighboring towns of Patzún, Santa Apolonia and Poaquil, and Santa Cruz Balanyá. Given Tecpán's location just off the Pan-American Highway, there are also buses running constantly both east toward the capital and west toward Quetzaltenango and the Mexican border. A few families in Tecpán occasionally make the trip to the *frontera*, buying goods for resale just over the border in Tapachula, Mexico.

Tecpán's bus service is remarkable not for its comfort but for its efficiency. It provides Tecpanecos with relatively quick and affordable connections to the rest of the country. But along with this possibility of mobility, Tecpanecos usually maintain strong ties to their community through a social umbilical cord that is painful and difficult to break. It is not uncommon for one or more members of a family to work in Guatemala City, Antigua, or more distant towns, either making the hours-long journey every day or sleeping over where they work and coming home on the weekends. This is difficult for families but is more often than not accepted as necessary to maintain family structure and community ties.

Although Tecpán is known for its relative economic prosperity in the region, upward mobility is often associated with working in Guatemala City or, at least, Chimaltenango, the departmental capital. Professionals in particular find it difficult to find work locally and therefore look to the larger towns or city for employment that will use their skills and pay a decent wage. Teachers, for example, are often assigned to work in distant communities, with teaching assignments com-

Figure 1.4   One of the distinctive red and white Poaquileña buses leaving Tecpán for Guatemala City. The ayudante *is leaning out of the door, whistling to let people know the bus is leaving town.*

ing from the centralized national education ministry. Here too individuals often commute rather than relocate because of difficult assignments. For instance, a woman from Tecpán who teaches school in a distant aldea rises at 3:30 every morning to prepare her family's breakfast before starting the two-hour bus ride and one-hour walk to her one-room school house; the trip back home in the afternoon is no shorter. What is more, the commute that allows her to live at home not only adds hours to her paid workday, but she retains her work at home as wife/mother and thus becomes a classic example of a woman with a "double day."

HEARTH AND HOME

For most Tecpanecos, the home symbolically represents and physically embodies the comfort and security of a refuge from the wider world. Indeed, the Kaqchikel language refers to the home as a metaphorical extension of the human body: for example, *ruchi' jay* ("mouth of the house") is the door, *ruwi' jay* ("hair of the house") is the roof, and *rupan jay* is the inside ("stomach of the house").

In urban spaces such as the *cabecera* of Tecpán, one home abuts the next, and the stuccoed front walls of individual houses press out to the very edge of the roads, giving the passerby little indication of what lies inside. Exceptions to this are the many homes that include small business spaces (as little as an 8 foot by 10 foot room) in the front where the family might have a tiny general store or run a bakery, pharmacy, or shop that sells meat, candles, threads, or school and stationery sup-plies. Here neighbors drop in to buy a manila folder or half dozen eggs and might pause to chat with the shop owner or another customer. Beyond this public/private area, it is common to find an open-air patio of packed earth, concrete, or tiles, which can serve as a parking space for a vehicle, a garden space for flowers and small fruit trees, a play yard for children, a drying area for corn or clothes, and an area in which a woman can work on her backstrap loom. A roofed corridor typi-cally lines one or more sides of the patio, with individual rooms radiating off this covered walkway. Closest to the road it is common to find a multi-purpose living room, a space for entertaining visitors that might also serve as a TV room, weaving or sewing space in inclement weather, storage area, or a shop. In Catholic homes it is not uncommon to find an altar space here, too. Bedrooms (often sleeping spaces for multiple people), a storage room, and dining area may follow, with the kitchen and then bathroom and a *pila* (a large sink with faucet and water storage areas, this often the only source of running water) at the farthest end. In these more out-of-the-way spaces, the family might also have specific areas for storing grain (hard corn still on the cob and perhaps feed for animals), firewood, and building supplies as well as a pen for a couple of chickens, a pig, or some rabbits. In some homes a *temescal*, or sweatbath, might be located in a far corner of the property. And in compounds that are home to more than one nuclear family, separate house spaces, or at least additional rooms, can be found on the same property.

Because the weather is always moderate, doors are left open during the day, making much less of a difference between inside and out than in homes in the United States, for example. What this means in terms of activity is that children run back and forth from patio to rooms with their soccer balls or toy soldiers, that the route to the bathroom is often wet in the rainy season, and that the corri-dor becomes a site of congregation and passing throughout the day.

At the symbolic if not necessarily physical center of the home is the kitchen and cooking hearth, sometimes referred to as *rute' q'aq'* ("mother of the fire"). In years past (and today still in some of the poorest homes), hearths were (and are) made from three stones (*xk'ub' q'aq'*) grouped around a small fire on the dirt floor. Meals were eaten around the hearthstones, and older Tecpanecos recall with fondness the conviviality brought about by sitting around the fire and shar-ing thoughts. Today, most homes have dining tables, which some elders see as un-conducive for family interactions.

Most households still cook with wood fires, but in adobe or cinder block stoves, most often placed to connect with a chimney built into the wall. The tops of these new stoves are made with a metal plate that has several removable circu-lar cooking tops. The fire is built underneath the cooking surface and accessible through a small side opening in the adobe construction. There are usually live coals in the stove, thus allowing a person to quickly stoke up active fires when something needs to be warmed or it's time to cook. An increasing number of households also have small propane stoves, which they use to cook a quick meal

Figure 1.5   Doña Pancha sitting next to her wood-burning brick stove in 1994. She has since replaced it with a propane gas stove.

or make a pot of coffee. There is a dignified stoicism to women's household work, and this is widely, if implicitly, acknowledged by most men. Women's esteem derives partly from the adverse conditions in which they work, hovering over the intense heat of the stove, for example, and exposing themselves to biting odors, such as from burnt chile.

Mealtime interactions are very important in Kaqchikel families and society. They are occasions when the family, and sometimes selected guests, can come together to discuss common problems and determine a next step or solution in a manner that generally values consensus and respect for elders. As anthropologists have noted in societies around the world, the act of sharing food oils the wheels of human interaction and, in stressing the conviviality of the human condition, creates an atmosphere conductive to empathetic understanding and in-group coherence (Goody 1982). Significantly, a visitor rarely leaves a Tecpán household without being plied with food, at the very least some sweat breads and a cup of coffee. Mealtime interactions

The Kaqchikel Kitchen

The kitchen in most Kaqchikel houses is at once dark and smoky and warm and inviting. Here women spend much of their day, as other family members come and go for meals, snacks, and conversation. Maize and beans form the staples of the Tecpán diet, and a perfectly adequate (and common) meal may include little else. At the same time, the Kaqchikeles have a rich culinary tradition. Tortillas are always the heart of the meal, and in addition to beans may be served a bit of meat (most often chicken, but some beef and pork as well), an egg, or some greens. Chile peppers are a staple condiment in the Maya diet, adding a bit of spice to these solid foods. Meals also usually include a rich variety of salsas, some very hot, some very mild, but all flavorful, blending tomato (either red tomatoes or small, husked green miltomates), cilantro, and chiles. After the start of the rains, succulent wild mushrooms with names like *rixk'eq xar* (claw of the Xar-bird), *raq' mazat* (deer tongue), and *runun tz'i'* (dog penis) appear in the market and grace tables for special occasions. The other seasons are likewise marked by the coming and going of different fresh vegetables and fruits: pitaya, avocados, fresh roasted corn on the cob.

in Tecpán also overtly mark relations of seniority. Individuals are served in order of their perceived status (a complex calculation that weighs age, sex, and social standing), and every meal time allows for reification—and renegotiation—of relative status. Ironically, it is usually the most junior individuals present (those serving the meal, perhaps even a servant from outside the family) who are charged with making clear individuals' relative rankings. More than once we have witnessed a confused young girl eyeing a table trying to decide whom to serve next.

The foods made and consumed in Tecpán run the gamut from the seemingly unexceptional though essential to the special and noteworthy treat. Virtually no meal in Tecpán would be complete without tortillas, an item whose preparation consumes vast amounts of Tecpán women's time each day and whose substance accounts for a good percentage of the calories and certain nutrients in a Tecpaneco's diet. To prepare tortillas, kernels of corn are removed from the dry ears stored in the granary and are then soaked in water and lime overnight (a process that can be speeded up by boiling the mixture). When the lime has sufficiently broken down the hard kernels, the mixture (called *nixtamal*) is ground into a dough (*masa*). If the *nixtamal* is ground by hand, it is passed over the *metate* (a grinding stone) three or four times to achieve a fine consistency. Most Tecpanecos take their *nixtamal* to one of the many neighborhood mills found throughout town as a substitute for the initial millings, but they then might still grind the resulting *masa* on the *metate* once more to achieve the required consistency for tortillas. The *masa* is then patted by hand into thin, round tortillas that are cooked on a hot griddle. From the griddle they are piled into baskets and wrapped in *servilletas*, then delivered to family members awaiting a meal. Many women make tortillas only once a day, relying on leftovers to be reheated or toasted for the other meals. Some also buy tortillas—most common for women with jobs outside the home and no female relative or maid to make them—when they simply don't have the time themselves.

If tortillas have a regular presence at highland meals so as to make their existence in Tecpán somewhat unexceptional, then the sausages produced there can be considered their opposite—a culinary item that is both a special treat and something for which the town is known. Meat is hardly common at every meal and, for poorer families, often nonexistent on a daily basis. Sausages, like ice cream and cake, are a special item that families might buy only occasionally, perhaps for a celebratory occasion. Tecpán is regionally famous for its sausages, and there are a number of sausage factories around town, most located in the backs of people's houses. Some sausage makers raise their own pigs; others buy their pork from local farmers or the large pig farm in town. Whatever the source of the raw material, they grind the meat themselves, spice it, and pack it into skins made from intestines. Then, depending on the type of sausage, it may be smoked for several days or even weeks. The results are short, plump sausages, with a large amount of gristle and fat, but with a noteworthy flavor known to people well beyond the borders of town. The sausage makers have used the fame of their product to spin off a growing subsidiary business of small meat stands and grills along the Pan-American Highway, serving the buses and tourists who pass by on their way to Lake Atitlán or farther into the highlands.

KINSHIP AND FAMILY LIFE

In places like Tecpán, kinship relations have been formalized by the Guatemalan government. Births and marriages must be registered in the town hall, wills must be probated by a judge, and deaths are duly recorded there. And yet long-standing local norms of kinship relations continue to serve important legal, political, and economic interests as well as crucial social functions.

In anthropological terms, contemporary Kaqchikel kinship is cognatic with a patrilateral bias. This is to say, that, like our own kinship system, Kaqchikeles consider themselves to be related to both their mother's relatives and their father's relatives. At the same time, there is a marked male bias in the system. Inheritance, for example, often follows male lines; children carry the surnames of both their mother and father, but the mother's name is lost at marriage (the wife takes her husband's surname instead) and birth (individuals pass on only their father's surname). Reinforcing this male bias, upon marriage, a woman commonly goes to live with her husband and his family.

Kaqchikel has a complex system of kinship terms that distinguishes both sex and relative age. For example, a person (Ego) uses the term *nunimal* to refer to an elder same-sex sibling (be it brother or sister) and *nuchaq'* to refer to a younger same-sex sibling. (*Nuchaq'* may also refer to the children of siblings, regardless of relative age or sex.) A male Ego uses a single term (*wana'*) to refer to a sister, regardless of her age, and a female Ego likewise uses *nuxib'al* to refer to all her brothers. Figure 1.6 shows a Kaqchikel kinship chart for a female Ego.

The study of kinship has a long history in anthropology, and kinship diagrams have been central to ethnographic sketches. Unfortunately such figures often seem esoteric, far removed from the real world relations upon which they are based and the way local people learn and understand these terms. So it is important to keep in mind that Kaqchikel kinship terms both reflect and condition the ways in which relatives interact with one another.[4] For example, the terms for siblings given above reinforce traditional familial authority just as they may be situationally used to renegotiate terms of familiar interaction. The first born child (*nab'ey alaxel*) in many Maya households quickly assumes certain duties of adulthood: sons making the transition from diapers to machetes (although use of this tool is now less common for boys in the town center) and daughters assuming many of the responsibilities of caring for younger siblings. The sacrifices of the older children are culturally recognized, and evident in the fact that younger children are more likely than their elder siblings to attend school and obtain good jobs. With this sacrifice comes both obligation and authority: an obligation to look out for the best interests of the family's children and the authority to impose their will as befits a care giver. It is also common for elder children to take an active role in the socialization of their same-sex siblings and thus promote the status of relative age among same-sex siblings through actions as well as kinship terminology.

What anthropologists call *fictive kinship* is also an important means of establishing social relations with individuals who are not blood relatives or related by marriage. *Compadrazgo* (literally "co-parenthood") offers a means to solidify ties with both relatives and non-relatives, principally for families that are not Protestant. Based on the Catholic tradition of having godparents, a person might have several sets of *padrinos* (godparents), the first and most important being the godparents of baptism, but then also for, say, a girl's fifteenth birthday and a couple's wedding. In selecting *padrinos* families consider individuals or couples with whom they are friends and who take on the charge of providing gifts on key occasions and in general looking out for the person or couple's well-being. In turn, the family asking for this relationship honors the *padrino* or *padrinos* with places of honor at celebratory occasions. *Padrinos* also give counsel to a person throughout his or her life.

Where kinship is most complexly and regularly played out is in the home. The number of family members residing in the same compound can be large. Two or

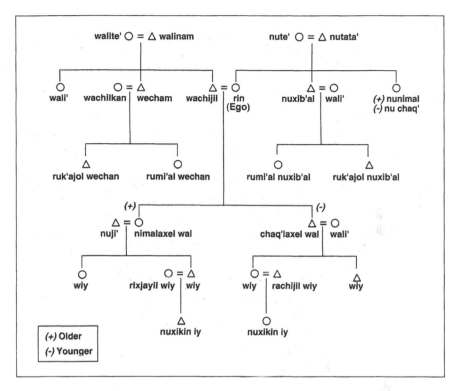

Figure 1.6   Kaqchikel kinship terms, married female Ego.

more related nuclear families often live together on the same property: in Tecpán, households have an average of 1.27 nuclear families and, with fertility rates of Guatemalan women one of the highest in the Americas (4.7 births per woman in 2000), families average over 6 members each. (For comparison, the United States averaged 2 births per woman in 2000, while Germany averaged 1.4.) What this means is that married children with children of their own regularly live next to or with their parents and perhaps siblings and siblings' families. What this also means is that at any given moment within the household there are large and small family "dramas"—tragedies and comedies and everything in between—unfolding and involving various members. To get a taste of these dynamics, we present two snapshots of family life. The first has to do with changes in family membership—the courtship and marriage of a couple—and the rituals that surround this. The second concerns the work of a wife and mother in a household, what she is told she should do, what she feels she can and can't do, and thoughts on negotiating this tension. Other chapters contain additional material on family life in Tecpán that complements and expands on this introductory material.

Courtship and Marriage

In years past, marriages were arranged by the parents of the young man and woman, taking into consideration the wishes of the youth. Marriage then was seen not so much as the flowering of some idyllic romantic love as a contract between two families, although that did not stop meaningful glances and comments between a couple with interests in each other or meetings in the market, at church, or along the road. This is not to say that love was absent from marriages of generations past, but that affective love was seen to develop as couples provided for each other's needs in a thoughtful, consistent way. Even today, in an era when couples may get to know prospective partners while in school or at work outside of Tecpán and marry for love and mutual interests a person their parents have only recently met, courtship can still be very circumspect and proceed without a great deal of public notice.

In traditional Kaqchikel marriages (meaning the idealized marriage of the past and ones today that aim to uphold Maya *costumbre* or custom), negotiations between the two families take place in a series of *pedidas* (requests), ritualized nighttime meetings at the home of the woman's family. These are arranged and mediated by a trusted intermediary (a *cholonel*) selected by the hopeful groom's family. The young man's family provides the *cholonel* with baskets of meat, tamales, liquor, soft drinks, candles, and incense to be given to the family of the prospective bride during the *pedidas*. In the past it was customary to have three *pedidas*, although today these are often truncated into a single meeting if not dispensed with altogether.

At the start of the most elaborate *pedidas*, the house is cleansed with incense to flush out any malevolent spirits. Protestant families might not perform such acts, which could seem too "Catholic" or close to "*brujería*" (witchcraft), substituting Christian prayer instead. Then the young man and his family will state their intentions to the family of the young woman with the guidance of the *cholonel*; the young woman herself will not be present. After an hour or more of addressing the hopes and concerns of both parties, the young woman will be invited in and asked to kneel with her suitor in front of the assembled families. At this time, the elders impart their views on marriage and entreat the couple to live up to their expectations; in turn the youths are expected to critically review their lives, with a particular focus on past misdeeds and how they have learned from their mistakes. If all goes well, a formal announcement of engagement will result, and plans for the wedding festivities will be initiated.

This description captures a sense of the ritual of courtship and preparations for marriage for a significant portion of couples in the past and even today. However, with the proliferation of churches in town (and hence the religious frames for the ceremony) plus changes in where young people meet each other (in schools and jobs) and who accumulates cash wealth (young people with salaried jobs more than their parents who work the land), "the old ways" can hardly stand unchanged. Along with variations in the *pedida*, people may simply introduce their prospective spouses to their families and begin wedding plans, church-sanctioned "Farewell to Youth" celebrations may be held prior to the wedding, or couples may simply elope.

For the majority of couples who are married in a public ceremony, the groom and his family typically provide the resources for the wedding celebrations, although nowadays some couples—especially ones with professional jobs—are paying for the wedding themselves and even splitting expenses. The groom and his family are responsible for providing the bride with her wedding *traje* (traditional dress) and, depending on the means of the family and the attitude of the family toward the bride, dress her in an outfit that provides material comment on their attitude toward the union. Who appears at the wedding and who doesn't provides insight into family relations, both within the bride's and groom's families and between the two families. For example, a mother of the groom might boycott the marriage ceremony or appear in church in old, dirty clothes as a way of expressing her disapproval of her son's marriage partner. Who is chosen as *padrinos* (in non-Protestant cases), who is included in the wedding party, how the families interact, and what kinds of celebrations follow the civil and church ceremonies all reflect ongoing family relations and the shifts that must be negotiated as family membership changes.

Wife and Mother

Although ceremonies like courtship and marriage are the highly public and focused rites of a society, everyday routines consume a much larger percent of a person's time and, in their own way, are no less reflective of "the big issues of life." An example of this is the daily work of being a wife and mother who is learning what is expected of her; doing what she feels she needs to do, knows how to do, and actually can do; considering what she can expect from other people; and calculating what concessions can and need to be made for the particular circumstances and personalities involved, all the while balancing a range of relationships with some combination of parents, siblings, a husband, in-laws, children, aunts and uncles, cousins, and/or hired help within a single or extended household.

A sense of these relations, expectations, and demands of life emerges in the comments of Doña Ramona, an eighty-four-year-old woman reflecting back on her life when her children were small and she was relatively new in the role of wife and mother. In this narrative (and we cannot know how things played out in actions long past), she begins by affirming her belief in the traditional role of women in Maya society (one that was taught to her and that she, in turn, taught to her daughter), but the manner in which she organizes her life story is one of successful resistance to what emerges as an inflexible and unworkable social ideal:[5]

> *I was taught to be obedient to my husband, to do what he said without asking questions. This is a wife's place, and this is how I taught my daughter to act as well. It was difficult. My husband would spend all of our money on drink, and I would have to make do on just a couple of quetzals*

every week, barely enough to buy salt, and usually not enough to buy soap as well. I began to weave again, as my mother had taught me. One day, while I was struggling with my husband and our condition, trying to feed our children, my mother called me to her house. She gave me two large balls of thread she had spun, enough with which to make a huipil. She told me that this was my little bit, that I should weave a huipil, sell it, and buy more thread with the money, and in this way I could have a few cents to provide for the family. But my husband did not want me to weave, not to sell in the market. So I hid when I did my weaving, and I would keep my backstrap loom set up in the corn barn, working in the dim light and corn dust. He found me one day and said, "what is this?" He was very angry, and ordered me to stop, but I continued. What else could I do? I had to care for my children.

Shifts and changes have always been part of social relations, and today is no exception. Words that Doña Ramona used to describe her upbringing in the first half of the twentieth century are true more than fifty years later. However, a couple of points should be considered when comparing this account of the past with the current situation. First, this is *one woman's* story, and she has ordered the myriad elements of the past and her experiences into this brief account. What has been told and what has been left untold? Second, the gender teachings described by Doña Ramona come across as being produced within and confined to the sphere of the family. That is probably largely true, but these no doubt also resonated with and contradicted teachings from other sources, including social messages from her family.

Today, messages about gender relations—the duties, obligations, and rights of women, for example—certainly emanate from multiple sources: the family (always), but also schools, the government, churches, nongovernmental organizations (NGOs) operating in the area, the media, and visiting anthropologists or other foreigners in town. These messages may deal with issues of legal rights, education, body image, or reproductive rights and present challenges to the definition of family and the roles of individuals within the family and beyond. Additional examples of these current issues are included later in this book.

RHYTHMS OF COMMUNITY

There is a rhythm to life in Tecpán that is palpable and made from the intermeshing of multiple cycles: daily, weekly, seasonal, political, ritual, biological, and more. Women are generally early to rise, with farmers' wives often stoking the fire and starting breakfast long before dawn. As men leave to tend their fields or go to their jobs, the women begin the many daily tasks of washing clothes and dishes, going to market, and preparing lunch, which is the primary meal of the day. At night the family reunites over dinner, often lingering round the table for hours in conversation. Whereas weekdays mean school and the work of fields and office jobs, weekends generally mean church, special outings, and more time with family. On late Wednesday afternoons, the normally tranquil town center converts into a hotbed of economic activity as the weekly market is set up. It becomes temporarily populated by thousands of people on Thursday mornings and then virtually disappears again by Thursday evenings.

October 4 is the saint's day for Francis of Assisi, Tecpán's patron saint. Religious and secular celebrations start well before that date and intensify during the week surrounding it, culminating in a grand town fiesta. The month of October also heralds an end to the six-month rainy season and the start of a long school vacation that lasts through the harvest season, until after the New Year. The moveable Holy Week feast (Semana Santa) in March or April again brings Tecpanecos to the streets for parades and general merriment, a prelude to the onset of the rainy season. Punctuating the celebrations of the Catholic annual calendar are native holy days (such as Waxaqi' B'atz, or 8 Monkey), which occur on a 260-day cycle and are marked by ceremonies conducted at home altars and holy spots in the hills around town.

The rains come and the rains go; the color of the world changes from brown to green to brown; and the majority of work that farmers must do—plant, weed, harvest—is dictated by these shifting seasons and climate patterns. Add to this the political cycles of campaign promises, elections, government initiatives, military build-ups, and the optimism and pessimism of the public-at-large syncopate with the brutal reality of Guatemala's political system (military violence and insurgent counterattacks, corruption, and service to the wealthy much more than the poor) as well as its social efforts (in support, for example, of Mayan language projects, bilingual education, and indigenous rights). State holidays such as the Día de la Raza (Race Day), Independence Day, and Army Day bring these grand social processes into temporary focus before they again fade into the background, less visible in daily life although no less influential.

TECPÁN, CIRCA 2000

When gathering materials for this book, we returned to Tecpán in 1999, 2000, and 2001. We were both struck by the rapid pace of change in town over the previous few years. Most visibly, there has been a boom in construction, both of large buildings and house additions. Visiting friends, it seemed that almost every family had a stack of masonry blocks and a pile of sand in their patio, supplies for their latest project. To date, two *centros comerciales* (shopping centers) have been built; one even houses a hotel that boasts satellite television, private baths, and hot water (a big step up from the Hotel Iximche', the best accommodations in town in the early 1990s). In 2000, the owner of a large propane tank factory opened an even more

Figure 1.7   The Plaza Tecpán, a two-story shopping center that opened on the central plaza in 2001. Note the two banks.

luxurious hotel. With stained glassed windows in the foyer and a fountain and garden in a lobby whose ceiling rises to the fourth floor rooftop terrace, the Villa de
Don Pancho has the hushed tones of understated privilege. The hotel offers not
only hot water at all hours but also a sauna and jacuzzi, a staff masseuse, and in-
room telephones for about US$30 per night. Given that local wages are about $3.30
a day, the hotel's prospects might seem dim, but in fact employees report that it is
frequently full, mostly with Guatemalans from the capital taking a vacation and the
occasional group of affluent cyclists or soccer players.

In 2000, two more *centros comerciales* were being built. Of these, the Centro
Comercial Plaza Tecpán will easily be the largest shopping center in town, with
thirty-one ground-level storefronts slated to be opened in the first phase and space
for an equal number on the second floor (which is being roughed-in but not finished). The Plaza Tecpán occupies a prime piece of real estate, abutting the town
hall and facing the central plaza; the site was formerly the home of the Ciné
Imperial and a family-run store, which closed in 1981 after its owner (a member of
a prominent local *ladino* family) was murdered; between 1981 and the late 1990s a
number of small stores operated out of the front rooms. With Tecpán's importance
as a regional trading center increasing, the family that owned the old building decided to tear it down and build the Plaza Tecpán. By 2001 the structure was complete, with several stores already open. What had created perhaps the greatest stir
around town concerning the building was a rumor that Pollo Campero (the coun-

Figure 1.8   The Café Internet Bohemios, which opened in Tecpán in 2001.

try's wildly popular fast food fried chicken chain) planned to open a location there; for many this would have been a true sign of the town's progress and its entry into the ranks of Guatemala's most important cities. Alas, it was not meant to be, although the center did manage to get a Pollolandia, a knockoff brand.

The list of changes goes on and on. There are now three full-service bank branches in Tecpán, and one even offers Western Union's services (allowing, for example, migrant workers living in the United States to wire money to their relatives at home). An Internet Café (Bohemios) opened in 2001 and was doing a brisk business that summer.

A second story has been finished on the town hall, bringing it back (in style and size) to the grandness of the colonial structure destroyed in 1976, and the town market building is also being expanded. There are more cars on the streets than ever before, and a fleet of more than ten taxis now serves the town (the first having appeared only in 1998).

Life for farmers in the countryside is changing as well, and many have mixed feelings about the direction of these changes. The flat plain of the Tecpán valley is well suited for maize and wheat farms, and during the colonial period (and up until just recently) Tecpán was an important source of the country's wheat flour. Indeed, beauty pageant contestants representing Tecpán have often appeared with sheaves on their arms and wheat in their crowns as a symbol of the town. Two mills still operate alongside the Río Molino (Mill River), which flows through the Tecpán valley, but they must truck in wheat bought in the capital because local farmers have virtually ceased to grow it. Wheat production throughout the country has declined by over 90 percent since 1990, with only 3,000 metric tons produced in 1999. Farmers we talked to in 1999 and 2000 all bemoaned chronically low wheat prices, and a few blamed the United States for flooding local markets with surplus wheat. (To bring itself into compliance with World Trade Organization mandates, in 1997 Guatemala lowered tariffs on wheat and wheat flour entering the country as well as dropping government price supports for basic grains; as a result, private sector wheat imports have doubled between 1997 and 2000.) Wheat was formerly rotated regularly with *milpa* by many farmers in the Tecpán area, who reported much higher yields from both crops using such rotation. Today, instead of wheat, many of these same farmers are planting nontraditional export crops such as broccoli, snow peas, and miniature vegetables. Production of maize, the staple food of Tecpán and all of Guatemala, has also declined since 1990, although not as dramatically, while maize imports have more than doubled over the same period. Again, many former subsistence maize plots have been converted to nontraditional production.

Figure 1.9   Fleet of taxis lined up along the central plaza.

Factors precipitating such changes are both external (the U.S. market for broccoli, for example) and internal (a post-violence willingness to stake a claim in

Tecpán's future), and they present new opportunities as well as imposing new restrictions on people's lives. As they have done for centuries, Tecpanecos (Kaqchikeles and *ladinos* alike) actively engage the outside world, selectively appropriating and resisting, accommodating and rejecting new ways of doing things. People's values and meanings in life are always in a state of flux, never solidifying into the neat structure anthropologists would like to document. But change is only half of the equation, for new strategies and ways of looking at the world are always informed by past experience, historical awareness, and the deeply embedded lessons learned in the lifelong process of socialization. Certain changes may be inevitable (say, the spread of television), but what these changes mean in people's lives is largely determined by cultural interpretation.

To understand Tecpán society today—and in particular what it is like for Tecpán Maya—it is first necessary to look at the broader context in which it exists. Guatemala's prolonged civil war and economic woes, combined with the near total devastation of the central highlands in the 1976 earthquake, have meant that Tecpanecos have had to deal with harsh political, economic, geological, and social realities that have shaped, although never completely determined, their daily lives.

Notes

1. The 1994 national census recorded 41,152 residents in the entire *municipio* of Tecpán, and 9,121 residents in the urban center. Given the rapid growth of the town in the late 1990s, 10,000 residents is a conservative estimate of the 2001 population.
2. This text uses the English word "Indians" for clarity.
3. The Guatemalan national currency is the quetzal, and its value in U.S. dollars fluctuates. Until 1984, the quetzal was on par with the dollar; by the mid–1990s the exchange rate had reached 6:1, and in the early 2000s it hovered around 8:1.
4. It is important to remember that not all indigenous people in Tecpán speak Kaqchikel—a few speak other Mayan languages while others are largely monolingual in Spanish; however, the sentiments carried by these Kaqchikel terms do not flow solely from language but rather from a complex of social phenomena that are differentially possessed by the various people in the community.
5. Large numbers of *ladino* brides hear virtually the identical charge concerning their husbands. How these charges get played out in different marriages and in different households—and what gets labeled as "Maya"—brings into play the whole set of circumstances of social life and cultural values of a community.

Further Reading

Fischer, Edward F. 2001. *Cultural logics and global economies: Maya identity in thought and practice.* Austin: University of Texas Press.

Hendrickson, Carol. 1995. *Weaving identities: Construction of dress and self in a highland Guatemala town.* Austin: University of Texas Press.

The local army base's float in the 2001 celebration of July 25th, the anniversary of Tecpán's founding by Pedro de Alvárado. The slogan reads "The Guatemalan Army: Protagonist of a New Thought."

2

The Guatemalan
Context

Classifying and Quantifying a Country and Its People

When Guatemala enters the popular imagination of North Americans, it is likely to be conceived as the home of impressive archaeological sites; a country recently ravaged by civil war; or a land of colorful textiles, puffing volcanoes, and impressive biodiversity. It is also a place of great human diversity. Publications of all sorts generally divide Guatemalan society into two major ethnic groups, Indians and *ladinos*, although there are smaller, but significant, populations of Garífuna, Chinese, Koreans, Germans, and people of other national origins. *Indígenas*, *naturales*, or *Maya'* are generally considered to be persons whose ancestors lived in the area in pre-Conquest times, have the ability to speak one of the country's twenty-one Mayan languages, use traditional dress, and/or self-identify as Indians. *Ladinos*, in turn, are widely defined by academics as non-Indians, persons of mixed descent who might be termed *mestizos* in other Latin American countries. They speak Spanish, wear Western clothes, and make a broad implicit claim to European descent. However, although others might label them "*ladino*," they rarely identify themselves using that term. The ideology of *mestizaje* has not taken hold in Guatemala as it has in some other Latin American countries (such as in Mexico, where it plays an important role in national discourse). Instead, "*ladinos*" may identify themselves simply as "Guatemalan" or, in certain elite social circles, as Spaniards or European to stress "blood purity" and the closeness of their ties to Europe and all that that means in terms of culture (or perhaps "Culture").

Terms for both of these major ethnic categories have multiple meanings that work both with and against their more common connotations. For example, the pejorative "*indio*"—often hurled at an indigenous person with great emotion and prejudice—is used by some Maya intellectuals as equivalent to the generic "*indí-*

gena," with the intention being to defuse the destructive power of the term just as some African-Americans use "nigger" in English. Similarly, among some non-Indian Guatemalan leftists it is fashionable to label themselves "*mestizo.*" This usage connotes a salubrious mixing of the best of two cultures (indigenous and Western) while providing non-Indians with a source of cultural pride at a time when many feel threatened by the resurgence of Maya culture in their country.

Census figures in Guatemala are problematic, and official government sources estimate the Maya population at about 40 percent, while Maya scholars and advocates frequently claim that the figure is 60 percent or more. Exact figures are hard to come by, complicated by difficulties in defining just what makes a person Indian or *ladino* and also by the politicized nature of population figures. Census figures are an important battle ground for contemporary Maya politics, with the prominent Maya activist Demetrio Cojtí claiming that the Maya peoples are the victims of statistical genocide, and that the more representative figure of 60 percent of the population should be used as a basis for affirmative action programs within the Guatemalan government. Complicating matters further, the categories of Indian and *ladino* are hotly contested by academics, politicians, and journalists, as well as negotiated in myriad daily interactions. *Ladinos,* generally speaking, control major government institutions, the military, and key economic sectors, which leads to the stereotype that *ladinos* are an oppressive class-cum-ethnic group (or ethnic group-cum-class); the other side of this equation equates Indians with poverty. And yet, statistically, most *ladinos* are poor, just as are most Indians. Guatemala has some of the highest poverty levels in the hemisphere, even though it has a moderately high per capita gross national product.

In the upper echelons of society, *ladino* elites are concerned with racial purity and, as mentioned above, a European biological heritage, important markers of class position. This is expressed in the importance of marrying within certain circles—something that gets played out publicly in wedding photographs and write-ups on the society pages of prominent national newspapers—and the elaborate genealogies that families maintain (see Casaús Arzú 1992). In popular usage Indian and *ladino* are employed as racial categories and spoken of using idioms of blood and descent as well as certain, often-damning, stereotypical "inherited characteristics" (e.g., being clever with their hands, exhibiting laziness). The vocabulary of race still pervades the national dialogue about what anthropologists consider "ethnic" issues: For example, October 12 in Guatemala is a national holiday celebrated as Día de la Raza (Race Day).

But a significant number of *ladinos,* especially poorer ones, are acculturated Indians, pointing to the fact that the categories of Indian and *ladino* are socially, rather than racially, defined in practice. People may abandon their identity as "Indian" through a process known as "passing." Passing usually involves a person or family moving away from the home community, mastering Spanish, using that language in the household, and perhaps marrying a self-identified *ladino* or *ladina.* Phenotypic features may call a person's *ladino* identity into question, and *cara de indio* ("face of an Indian") is sometimes used as a pejorative.

Table 2.1   Key Development Indicators for Guatemala and the United States

	Guatemala	United States
Life expectancy at birth	64.4	76.8
Literacy rate	67%	>99%
Access to potable water	68%	>99%
Access to electricity	65%	>99%
Telephone lines (per 1,000 people)	41	661
Internet hosts (per 1,000 people)	0.08	112.8

SOURCE: 1998 Data from the United Nations Development Program, www.undp.org.

The material reality of this situation of pronounced cultural differences is that a small percentage of the *ladino* population wields disproportionate power within Guatemala's political and economic systems. Guatemala is not a poor country; it consistently shows more impressive economic growth than neighboring Honduras, El Salvador, and Nicaragua. And yet a large percentage of its population lives in poverty. For example, according to figures produced by the United Nations Development Programme (UNDP 2000), some 87 percent of the population lives in poverty, with 67 percent of these people in extreme poverty, defined as income below what is needed for minimal subsistence levels and caloric intake. Thus the problem of poverty in Guatemala is not so much one of wealth as of inequality.

One measure used to gauge inequality is the Gini index, which ranges from 0 in hypothetical situations of perfect equality to 1 in like cases of perfect inequality. Although the data with which this index is calculated may be poor, nonexistent, or vary from source to source within a given country, a score below .450 is generally taken to indicate a healthy distribution of resources. According to World Bank statistics, in the developed world scores range from .401 for the United States to .252 for Norway to 0.195 for the Slovak Republic. At the other end of the scale is Guatemala, with a score of .596, exceeded in some calculations only by Brazil (.601) and Sierra Leone (.629).[1] More troubling still is that Guatemala's Gini index has increased dramatically over the last fifty years. In 1948, estimates placed it as low as .423, rising to .4972 in 1979, to .5826 in 1987, and to .596 in 1989. World Bank data from 1989 report that in Guatemala the lowest 20 percent of the population earned only 2.1 percent of all income, while the highest 20 percent earned 63 percent of income (see Table 2.1).

In the economic geography of Guatemala, poverty indicators rise significantly the farther away from the capital one travels. In this rough geography, Tecpán lies on the border between the wealthier "core" departments around Guatemala City and the increasingly impoverished, and Indian populated, areas to the west (see Lutz and Lovell 1990).

One of the most commonly used measures of economic development is gross national product (GNP)—the total market value of all goods and services produced by a country within a given period—and, in GNP per capita rankings, Guatemala consistently places in the upper end of developing countries. But GNP figures simply record gross totals of economic transactions, valuing none over another, when in fact not all economic exchanges contribute equally to development: Making hoes, for example, is surely more beneficial that making cocaine, although selling the equivalent of $1,000 of each would contribute equally to a country's GNP. Likewise, GNP fails to account for the long-term value of unused resources. If Guatemala were willing to increase its GNP at any cost, it could log as much of its tropical forests as possible, selling off the wood to make furniture and paper for the rest of the world, and replacing the forests with cattle ranches. But moving this great resource to the credit column of balance sheets this year would deny Guatemala the much greater long-term potential the tropical forests hold. Finally, and most significant in terms of its utility as a measure of development, GNP does not take into account the sorts of inequality recorded by the Gini index, namely social aspects of the human condition.

A more inclusive and nuanced measure of development has been developed by the United Nations Development Programme (UNDP), which annually publishes the *Human Development Report* with its Human Development Index (HDI). Responding to criticism that the GNP and other such indicators often miss social and political inequality, the HDI takes into account various measures of economic and social well-being, including income levels, literacy rates, education levels, and life expectancy. Using 1998 data, Guatemala ranks 120 out of 174 countries included in the HDI list. This is the lower end of what the UNDP categorizes as a "medium" level of development. Using HDI measures for the twenty-two departments in Guatemala, the Department of Chimaltenango, where Tecpán is located, rates 0.438 on a 0–1 scale, placing it two-thirds of the way down the list (see Table 2.2).

This situation of marked economic inequality with clear ethnic correlations fosters tensions within the country. There has long been a salient fear among *ladinos* that Indians would one day lead an uprising to reclaim their ancestral lands (see Nelson 1999); Indians too have rich oral traditions of resistance. In 1992, at the time of the Quincentenary celebrations of the Columbian encounter, some *ladinos* noted that the Moors had ruled the Iberian Peninsula for 500 years before the Spaniards were able to complete their *Reconquista*, implying that this too could be the fate of *ladino* Guatemalans. Similar fears, common in post-colonial situations where an ethnic minority controls a large portion of the productive resources, were called upon in Guatemala to justify state-sponsored terror campaigns in the civil war of the 1970s and 1980s. The rhetoric reflects a modernist dream of many Guatemalan elites, who would like to see their country be-

Table 2.2   HDI Ranking of Guatemala and Chimaltenango (1990s Data) among Selected Other Countries (1998 Data) and Guatemalan Departments.

Country	HDI	Rank	Department	HDI	Rank
Canada	.935	1	Guatemala	.829	1
USA	.929	3	Quetzaltenango	.464	8
Brazil	.783	74	Chiquimula	.446	13
Guatemala	**.619**	**120**	**Chimaltenango**	**.438**	**16**
Haiti	.440	150	Sololá	.391	19
Sierra Leone	.252	174	Alta Verapaz	.355	22

SOURCE: Human Development Report 2000 (UNDP 2000); Guatemala: El Rostro, Rural del Desarrollo Humano (UNDP-Guatemala 1999).

come a more culturally homogenous nation-state on the model of Western Europe and enjoy the fruits of progress that such a shift would entail. However, such fantasies became a living nightmare for Maya peoples touched by the violence, as the civil war worked to wipe out their culture as well as family members, homes, and some 440 villages.

Despite the yearnings and pretensions—not to mention the economic resources—of certain elite *ladino* sectors, Guatemala as a whole is lumped with other poor countries—the "Third World," or, in more current terminology, "lesser developed countries"—in the global discourse of development that was born after World War II (Escobar 1995). To distinguish the nation on the world stage and to set themselves apart as unique, Guatemalans ironically turn to their country's Maya heritage. Certain visual markers of indigenous identity are used repeatedly in national contexts, thereby reinforcing the message that "Maya" means "Guatemala" and makes the country unique. For example, the tourist brochures produced by the state-run Guatemalan Tourist Institute (INGUAT) pull heavily on the country's indigenous heritage to sell it to would-be visitors. Posters and pamphlets display the country's magnificent archaeological sites alongside pictures of textile-filled tourist markets, giving the message that Maya history and culture are Guatemalan history and culture. Guatemalan candidates in the Miss Universe pageants are always *ladinas*; however, they also always appear in the national costume section of the competition wearing particularly beautiful and elaborately crafted Maya dress. And athletes representing Guatemala in regional and international competitions regularly sport team outfits made entirely or partially of fabric the design of which says "Indian." Many

Maya complain that the state appropriates their image while giving no recompense to the Maya peoples themselves. These activists see this as the worst sort of hypocrisy: racists promoting stereotypical images to the world to enrich themselves by maintaining a system of oppression of Maya peoples.

A TURBULENT PAST

Modern Guatemalan history is dominated by conflict between Indians and *ladinos*, between rich and poor, between the state and guerrilla insurgents, as well as within families and communities. In 1944 a coup that deposed the dictator Jorge Ubico led to the country's first democratic elections and ushered in the period that is called "Ten Years of Spring" in Guatemalan political history. The army officers leading the coup were liberal democrats in the old-fashioned Enlightenment sense of the term—committed to the ideas of progress and development and pursuing their realization through economically liberal state policies. In 1954 a CIA-led coup put an end to the Ten Years of Spring after the government of Jacobo Arbenz began to expropriate unused lands owned by the powerful U.S.-based United Fruit Company. The 1954 coup marked the start of a string of right-wing leaders, most from the military, who garnered and increased their power within the Guatemalan state by fighting those opposed to their policies and vigorously protecting the broad interests of the large land owners and industrialists.

By the early 1960s, inspired by Fidel Castro's successful 1959 revolution in Cuba, a Marxist guerrilla resistance had broken out in the east of Guatemala, an area populated mostly by *ladino* peasants. The army, backed by the government and bolstered by U.S. assistance, overreacted to the threat in what would become a characteristic response, attacking communities and initiating a state of siege in which many people were implicated as subversives or collaborators. By 1968 the incipient rebellion had been crushed and the power of the military in fighting internal enemies greatly increased. The guerrillas dispersed and went underground, reemerging in the mid–1970s in the Indian-dominated western highlands.

Guatemalan insurgents were bolstered—morally, ideologically, and economically—by the successful 1979 Sandinista revolution in Nicaragua. But the Guatemalan military, backed by the largesse of the United States, responded by escalating the conflict even further, kidnapping and torturing thousands of suspected subversives (a broad category that could include almost anyone: school teachers, cooperative members, priests), destroying hundreds of entire *aldeas*, and killing tens of thousands of civilians. The U.S. government, mindful of Guatemala's location in its "backyard," feared that the Sandinista victory would set off a domino effect of communist revolutions in Central America, El Salvador and Guatemala both being particularly vulnerable.

Guatemala's violence reached its height in 1982–1983 under the rule of General Efraín Ríos Montt, a fervent evangelical Protestant who was not afraid of

Anthropologists and the War in Guatemala

People who conduct research in local communities (including communities in exile) quite naturally develop strong ties and a sense of deep obligation to the people whose lives they study. They are often well positioned to record and comment on human rights abuses in "marginal" areas of the world, speaking for those whose voices have less power to be heard. In addition, individuals who have lived through the violence as members of communities-under-attack provide unique first-person accounts and further contributions to a larger sense of history than any one person can provide. During the violence in Guatemala of the 1980s, several works played an important role in bringing to light the atrocities that were happening there. Of particular note are the collaborative effort of Rigoberta Menchú and Elisabeth Burgos-Debray (1984), *I, Rigoberta Menchú*; Robert Carmack's (1988) *Harvest of Violence*; and Victor Montejo's (1987) moving *Testimony: Death of a Guatemalan Village*.

More recently, teams of forensic anthropologists have begun excavating and studying the sites of massacres carried out in the 1980s. The work began in 1991 when forensic anthropologist Clyde Snow, along with local human rights groups and the Argentine Forensic Anthropology Team, helped found the Guatemalan Forensic Anthropology Foundation (FAFG). Their largest project to date has focused on massacres in three villages near the town of Rabinal: Chichupac (8 January 1982), Rio Negro (13 February 1982), and Plan de Sanchez (18 July 1982). After potential sites are identified, work begins by interviewing local residents about past massacres: Who was killed? When? How? By whom? Where were they buried? Excavations are then carried out at clandestine grave sites using standard archaeological methods, recording the stratigraphy and exact position of all artifacts and skeletal remains recovered. The artifacts, which may include pieces of clothing, personal papers, and bullets, are catalogued and taken to a lab for examination. Skeletal fragments and dental remains are pieced together in the lab, and the forensic anthropologists try to assign a cause of death (most often bullet or machete wounds, but sometimes smashed skulls or incineration) and come to some conclusions about how and by whom the massacre was carried out. Bullets often provide the crucial clue: The preferred weapon of the Guatemalan army was the Israeli-made Ghalil rifle, while the guerrillas most often used AK–47s. Such work has obvious political implications, as Guatemalans try to come to terms with their recent violent past *(continued)*

Anthropologists and the War in Guatemala

(continued from page 31) and assign some sort of formal blame to those responsible. Just as important, however, this work brings a partial closure for survivors whose lives have been torn apart by the violence, resolving lingering doubts about the fates of loved ones, vindicating eyewitness accounts of the violence, and allowing formal burials to finally take place. Find out more about forensic anthropology in Guatemala on this book's website.

---

using the sword to strike down his enemies. In a country with a clear Catholic majority, he brought to his rule the fervor of a man who believes he has God on his side. He was infamous for his catchy slogans for brutal campaigns. For example, his "beans and bullets" program referred to the rewards (food and social services) that members of communities in the central war zones would receive for their service as members of the poorly armed civil patrols working under army orders to sweep for guerrillas (Carmack 1988). Ríos Montt was also open to mixing God with politics to get international support. A member of the California-based Church of the Word, known as "Verbo" in Guatemala, Ríos Montt appeared on U.S. television evangelist Pat Robertson's Christian talk show a week after the coup and, during that appearance, Robertson pledged to raise $1 billion for the Guatemalan cause (Garrard-Burnett 1998: 140, 157); in the end, U.S. evangelical groups sent only $20 million to Guatemala while Ríos Montt was in office. Ríos Montt also assumed office while receipt of U.S. foreign assistance was still linked to a country's human rights conditions (a legacy of Jimmy Carter's presidency). Given Guatemala's abysmal human rights record, U.S. arms sales had been slowed, if never actually cut, in the late 1970s and early 1980s; however, more cordial relations between the Ríos Montt and Reagan administrations enabled the latter to unilaterally lift the arms embargo in 1983 (Jonas 1991: 195–199). The early 1980s then was a period of shifts in the presidential offices and administrations in both the United States and Guatemala, with the interests of each working—sometimes together, sometimes at odds—to produce lasting and often devastating effects on the lives of people in the highlands area.

In August 1983, after just seventeen months in power, Ríos Montt was deposed by more moderate factions within the army. General Oscar Mejía Víctores became president and in 1984 presided over the country's first truly free elections since 1950. Vinicio Cerezo, a moderate-liberal Christian Democrat who had lived for years in exile, assumed office in 1986, famously admitting on the eve of his election that his role as president was still very limited by the real power held by the military high command. Jorge Serrano Elías, a neoliberal businessman, conservative Protestant, and candidate of the right, was elected president in a 1991 run-off characterized by high absenteeism. He had promised grand economic reforms but was unsatisfied with the pace of change. Thus, in February 1993, Serrano, mimicking a recent move by Peruvian President Alberto Fujimori, conducted a self-coup in which he disbanded Congress and the Constitutional Court and gave himself broad powers. Serrano, however, seriously misinterpreted the country's political climate, and within two months an unlikely coalition of leftists, unions, businessmen, Maya groups, and the military leadership forced him into exile in Panama, where he is reported to be living a life of luxury after coming into office nearly bankrupt. In an equally surprising turn of events, Ramiro de León Carpio, then the government's human rights ombudsman, was elected by Congress, with the military's explicit blessing, to continue Serrano's term. Contrary to the high hopes that his election raised, reports of human rights violations (to both the government Office of the Human Rights Ombudsman and the Catholic Church's Human Rights Office) sharply increased during de León Carpio's rule. Furthermore, de León Carpio refused to disband the notorious civil patrol system, which the military supported but which de León Carpio himself had criticized while human rights ombudsman. In 1995, Alvaro Arzú—former mayor of Guatemala City with close ties to business interests, candidate of the right-wing Party of National Advancement (PAN), and a staunch proponent of neoliberal reforms—was elected president. His greatest achievement was overseeing the signing of a final peace accord with rebel forces in December 1996. The peace accords, however, required a large number of constitutional changes; when presented to the electorate in May 1999 (in a very confusing set of four yea-or-nay propositions), all were defeated.

Following run-off elections in January 2000, Alfonso Portillo, a candidate for the Guatemalan Republican Front (known by its Spanish acronym, FRG), was elected president. This was his second run for the Guatemalan presidency—he had narrowly lost the election to Arzú five years earlier—yet the loss in 1995 and the run-off in 2000 were hardly the only twists or stumbling blocks in the political trajectory of Portillo or the party he represented. The history of this man and his party will give a sense of the complex nature of Guatemalan politics today, a politics of wealthy individuals, political reincarnations, shadowy pasts, and endless promises to a population already jaded by its own experiences with politicians.

Perhaps surprisingly given Portillo's current position in the right-wing FRG, his early political efforts were as a leftist student activist. As was true of thousands of Guatemalans who spoke out against their government during the civil war, Portillo went into exile. He moved to Mexico, where he continued his student involvement and, in 1982, killed two men who were members of a rival political group. He claims he shot them in self-defense; others claim that he shot them without provocation. What seems certain is that, when he moved to another region in Mexico, the police did not follow him, and in 1995 the statute of limitations on criminal charges expired. In the late 1980s Portillo returned to

Guatemala and was elected to Congress in 1990 on the ticket of the moderate-liberal Christian Democratic (DC) party. His political views continued to change and, following an election scandal involving DC leadership, Portillo defected to the FRG, a party founded by ex-dictator Efraín Ríos Montt and closely associated with Guatemala's far right.

The FRG began as a political vehicle for Ríos Montt, the evangelical Protestant general who was head of state after the March 1982 coup d'etat. Leading the FRG ticket, he started campaigning for president in the 1994 elections, although he was ultimately disbarred by the Supreme Electoral Commission under a clause that forbids former dictators from becoming president. Before withdrawing from the election, he led in most of the polls, a fact attributed to his image as a law and order candidate in times of increasing street and other nonpolitical crime. Barred from running for president in 1995, Ríos Montt ran for Congress instead (emerging as the assembly leader) and tapped Portillo (who allegedly had romantic ties to the general's daughter) to run in his stead. Mr. Portillo lost by a mere 30,000 votes to Alvaro Arzú, whose principal assets seemed to be support from the huge Guatemala City population plus the perception that he was already so rich he would have no need to steal from the government. (It is not uncommon for Guatemalan leaders to amass large fortunes while in office; former President Vinicio Cerezo is known for writing long, self-reflective letters to the editor from the back deck of his yacht as it cruises the Caribbean Sea.)

The FRG has proven to be an intriguing party and one which attracts the most unlikely followers. Its popularity alone is odd to many observers, being the party of a dictator responsible for so many atrocities. And yet Ríos Montt's reign is best remembered as a time of low street crime, which it was, with many suspected criminals routinely executed on the spot. There seems to be an odd amnesia about the massacres that occurred under his watch, and when people do speak of the violence the name of Lucas García (Ríos Montt's predecessor) is mentioned much more often than that of Ríos Montt. Still, it is surprising that along with several other congressional candidates linked to human rights abuses during the violence, the country's former humans rights ombudsman and interim president, Ramiro de Leon Carpio, also ran for Congress on the 1999 FRG ticket.

INTERPRETING THE NEWS FROM GUATEMALA

News stories from Guatemala are notoriously difficult to interpret, and networks of communication in Guatemala are ill developed. For example, in 1994 a telephone relay tower outside of Tecpán was blown up, interrupting phone service to a large part of the western highlands. On its face, and as the national newspapers covered it, it was a typical guerrilla attack against state property: high visibility with minimal risk. An alternative and equally plausible interpretation, however, held that army soldiers, perhaps dressed as insurgents, carried out the attack to bolster their claims that army funding should not be cut as the civil war was winding down. What really happened? We will likely never know.

Guatemalan Heads of State Since 1974

1974–1978	General Kjell Laugerud García—won over Efraín Ríos Montt with the widespread assumption of voter fraud
1978–1982	General Romeo Lucas García—stepped up the army's counterinsurgency campaign to all-out war against guerrillas and villages suspected of collaborating with the insurgents
1982–1983	General Efraín Ríos Montt—seized power from Lucas García in a palace coup and accelerated the war during his seventeen months in power
1983–1986	General Oscar Mejía Víctores—led a counter-coup against Ríos Montt and then worked to return Guatemala to a civilian government.
1986–1991	Vinicio Cerezo—first civilian elected president since 1966; introduced modest reforms in government, but the military establishment remained outside his control
1991–1993	Jorge Serrano Elías—won a presidential election in which well below half the eligible voters cast valid ballots; after two years in office he staged a short-lived "auto-coup"
1993–1995	Ramiro de León Carpio—Human rights ombudsman elected by Congress under the close watch of senior military officials to complete Serrano's term
1995–2000	Alvaro Arzú—elected on a platform of broad neoliberal reform, his term was marked by the divestment of several state businesses (including the telephone company, Guatel)
2000–	Alfonso Portillo—candidate of the FRG party elected amid speculation about his relationship to and independence from Ríos Montt

Such ambiguity is not uncommon. In 1996, then-U.N. Secretary General Boutros Boutros-Ghali was scheduled to make a short visit to Guatemala to show his support for the peace process, which was advancing under U.N.-led mediation. As his official plane approached Guatemala, the military air traffic controllers guided it in. But rather than sending him to La Aurora International airport in Guatemala City, where his motorcade awaited him, Boutros-Ghali's plane was sent to a small dirt airstrip some 30 miles outside the capital. Perhaps it was an error, as the army claimed, a misunderstanding admittedly not outside the realm of quotidian possibilities in Guatemalan life. Or, as many Guatemalan observers saw it, maybe the military was slyly flexing its muscle, underlining the autonomy and sovereignty of the country while expressing a distrust of the U.N.

and its ongoing peacekeeping efforts in the country. It is precisely such indeterminacy that makes expressions of state disapproval—everything from daily hassles to terrorism—so effective. The intent is subtle enough to be deniable, but not too subtle that the message is obscured. In Boutros-Ghali's case, hours after his motorcade found the landing strip and whisked the Secretary General into the capital, a car bomb exploded just outside the presidential palace while he and President Ramiro de León Carpio conferred over dinner.

Such stories coming out of Guatemala border on the surreal. At times they seem as if they might be scenes lifted from the pages of a magical realist novel, a literary genre with deep roots in Latin America.

Like magical realism, the *testimonio* is a literary genre characteristic of Latin America, one that has effectively been used to convey the subjective horrors of state violence, the mundane routine of everyday life, and the disquieting juxtaposition of the two. More personal and more focused than conventional autobiographies, as their name suggests, *testimonios* are testaments, often moving firsthand accounts of specific events. The most famous contribution to the *testimonio* genre came from the collaboration of Elisabeth Burgos-Debray and a young K'iche' Maya woman, Rigoberta Menchú. In 1983 they published a transcribed and edited version of Menchú's autobiographical oral history. *I, Rigoberta Menchú* is a powerful account of life in the rural surroundings of Uspantán, a small town located in an area hit particularly hard by the violence in Guatemala. Menchú and Burgos-Debray (who transcribed and substantially edited more than twenty hours of Menchú's spoken account) juxtapose accounts of a poor but not unhappy life before the violence with graphic descriptions of the horrors witnessed during the war. The story told is compelling, often heart-wrenching, and was certainly believable. These sorts of atrocities were happening in Guatemala, and because of her personal experiences Menchú was able to describe them and their effects in a particularly moving way. That the prose is often choppy and the chronology is sometimes unclear only added a luster of indigenous authenticity and played to the desires of Westerners to possess and consume the perceived purity of native experience. In 1992, the year of the Columbian Quincentenary, Rigoberta Menchú was awarded the Nobel Peace Prize.

Many college teachers have assigned *I, Rigoberta Menchú* in classes both to rid students of any lingering belief that the seemingly marginalized societies anthropologists study are somehow isolated from larger world events and to humanize the tragedies of state-sponsored violence. In this way the book became an icon of multiculturalism and a lightning rod for those opposed to curricular reform. Assigning it to students became a tool of subversion for teachers seeking to upset an established canon dominated by the ubiquitous dead white males and introduce new perspectives (non-white, non-Western, non-male) into core teaching areas. Menchú's book (Burgos-Debray is almost forgotten here) fits neatly into alternative pigeonholes: a powerful testimonial written by a young Maya woman refugee

Magical Realism and Reality

Magical realism refers to a narrative technique characteristic of a Latin American literary genre that blurs the distinction between reality and fantasy. It is probably best known through the works of Gabriel García Marquez, Isabel Allende, and Mario Vargas Llosa. Guatemalan novelist and diplomat Miguel Angel Asturias, who won the Nobel Prize for Literature in 1967, pioneered this approach in such works as *El Señor Presidente* (1946) and *Hombres de Maíz* (1949). In these novels, Asturias juxtaposes elements borrowed from Maya mythology with thinly veiled political satire to surreal (or, perhaps, hyper-real) effect; his goal, as stated in his Nobel lecture, was to create literature "with imponderable magical value and profound human projection." While Asturias is credited with valuing indigenous culture in his novels, contemporary Maya critics point to the modernist, eugenic sympathies expressed in his 1923 law school thesis, "Guatemalan Sociology: The Social Problem of the Indian." (Asturia's son became a prominent commander in the revolutionary forces of the 1980s.) Among recent works on Guatemala, Francisco Goldman's *The Long Night of the White Chickens* (1992) stands out in using magical realism to effectively capture the ambiguities and uncertainties of Guatemalan life.

As a literary genre, magical realism rejects simple narrative progression, preferring to juxtapose different perspectives--—often through dreamy, surrealistic interludes—to offer a more holistic view of a situation. Anthropologist Nancy Scheper-Hughes notes that "the magical realism of Latin American fiction has its counterparts in the mundane surrealism of ethnographic description, where it is also difficult to separate fact from fiction, rumor and fantasy from historical event, and the events of the imagination from the events of the everyday political drama" (1992: 229). (See also Clifford 1988; Marcus and Fischer 1986.) If, as some claim, all culture may be treated as a sort of text, then ethnography may fruitfully be considered a form of literature. Diane Nelson (1999) playfully calls ethnography a type of "science fiction," composed of stories based in fact (which gives the work an air of scientific exactitude) but self-consciously crafted and selectively edited stories all the same. Perhaps, then, the magical realism of Latin American literature can point us toward useful alternatives in our quest to more vividly represent the lives of those we study.

with little or no formal education whose descriptions of the human effects (and causes) of violence effectively refute abstract Cold War political justifications for fighting communism in Guatemala.

In 1998, anthropologist David Stoll published *Rigoberta Menchú and the Story of All Poor Guatemalans,* in which he questions the veracity of events written about in *I, Rigoberta Menchú.* In the course of several years of research for another book he was writing about violence in the K'iche' region, Stoll found a number of troubling inconsistencies between what appeared in *I, Rigoberta Menchú* and how some of Menchú's relatives and compatriots remembered events. For example, Stoll claims that Menchú was better educated at the time of her exile than she maintained, that the violence her family suffered was precipitated more by internecine struggles over land than by inter-ethnic conflicts, and that the famous incident Menchú described of her brother being burned to death by soldiers in the town square never happened. Stoll makes clear that such things as violent deaths at the hands of soldiers and inter-ethnic land disputes did happen in Guatemala at the time, pointing to the fundamental validity (if not precise veracity) of Menchú's account. Indeed, that Menchú's story went unquestioned for so long points to its plausibility (even to experts in the field) in representing the effects of violence on individuals and communities.

One of the more inflammatory responses to Stoll's revelations was a *Wall Street Journal* editorial by Stephen Schwartz published on December 28, 1998, entitled "A Nobel Prize for Lying." Schwartz writes of "the hoax" revealed by Stoll and attacks "Ms. Menchú's liberal apologists" and "the Marxist guerrilla movement that wreaked havoc on Guatemala for decades." Schwartz writes in a style reminiscent of Holocaust revisionist studies, and he compares *I, Rigoberta Menchú* with Binjamin Wilkomirski's memoir of Nazi atrocities, which has been proven fictional. Schwartz and others make the overly simple and misleading assumption that because parts of Menchú's account are of questionable veracity then the whole work and what it stands for should be rejected outright; however, that Ms. Menchú's brother was not murdered in the way that she described does not change the fact that thousands were murdered and tortured under almost unimaginable circumstances. Similarly, David Horowitz, writing in *Salon* online magazine,[2] jumps to the conclusion that "virtually everything that Menchú has written is a lie." Horowitz lays blame on "the cultural power of the perpetrators of this hoax" and those who continue to "defend her falsehoods." Such headlines must make Stoll cringe, for he is by no means a Guatemalan Holocaust revisionist, and yet he laid himself open to such reductionist misunderstandings through his representational strategy of (seemingly) letting the facts speak for themselves.

The U.S. popular media's black-and-white readings of selected issues in Stoll's work overlook the more profound questions raised about social truths, objectively valid representations of history, and people's differential access to public hearings via books. In its Spanish version, Menchú's book is titled *Me llamo Rigoberta Menchú y asi me nació la conciencia.* More tellingly than the English-language title, this means *My Name Is Rigoberta Menchú and Thus Was Born My*

Awareness, with *conciencia*/awareness referring to a political consciousness. While her book is perhaps more read in the United States than in Guatemala (not just in terms of sheer numbers but also in terms of the percentage of population), Rigoberta Menchú is well-known in Guatemala, and opinions abound about her. Thus, the appearance of the Stoll book led to a flurry of commentary in the Guatemalan press by a handful of people with the ability to read it in English. (A common comment about those who reacted to the Stoll book, both in the United States and Guatemala, was that sometimes it was not clear if the person commenting had actually read all—or even large parts—of the book.)

To a significant degree the comments in the Guatemalan press focused on the same issues found in the U.S. press, namely questions of veracity and the nature of what happened—to whom and perpetrated by whom—during the civil war. In the Latin American tradition *testimonios* often make use of composite representations (personalized in the voice of the narrator), and Menchú's story may be understood as a composite sketch of the violence in Guatemala. (Stoll mockingly points out that it was to be "the story of all poor Guatemalans.") Such composite representations may be used as a conscious representational strategy—a feeling, say, of being the rare person with the opportunity to be heard—or more subtly enter into texts through the processes of memory commingling, in which stories that one hears over time become inextricably linked to one's own personal experiences. Diane Nelson (1999) argues that press reports of Stoll's work assume an overly simplistic notion of truth and validity. She writes that "one does not have to be a post-modernist to know that the binary of true or not true may not always be clear cut, and may actually impoverish our understanding of complex realities." *I, Rigoberta Menchú* is likely to continue to be widely read and assigned in courses precisely because of its effectiveness in telling the larger truth of the Guatemalan violence as well as posing important questions about representations of history.

THE MURDER OF BISHOP JUAN GERARDI

On the night of April 26, 1998, Archbishop Juan Gerardi was murdered in the garage of his parish house at San Sebastián Church in Guatemala City. Gerardi had just driven home after a family gathering and was attacked as he left his car; he was bludgeoned to death with an eight pound block of concrete, leaving his face so mutilated that family members had to identify the body based on a distinctive ring Gerardi always wore. That he was killed is certain, but beyond this basic fact all else is murky regarding the case. The crime scene was investigated on the night of the murder and over the following days by a hodgepodge of Guatemalan security forces, including the National Police, prosecutors from the Public Ministry, and military intelligence officers from the notorious Presidential Guard. Well after the event, the FBI was allowed to go over the garage and offer technical assistance, but the scene had already been contaminated. On the night of the murder, evidence had been gathered haphazardly: Blood-stained clothing found at the scene was thrown into old boxes, the presumed murder weapon was handled without gloves, some evidence was taken by the special prosecutor and other items went with the National Police (compromising the chain of custody on which a future trial could well hinge), and dozens of officials milled around the body (leaving bloody footprints) before photos could be taken. And then less than twelve hours after the murder the crime scene was meticulously washed and cleaned of remaining evidence.

As a bishop, Gerardi had presided over the Diocese of El Quiché, a region devastated by the civil war, during some of the most intense violence. After receiving several serious death threats, presumably because of his concern with human rights abuses by the military in his diocese, Gerardi went into exile for several years. He returned to Guatemala to head the Human Rights Office of the Archbishop of Guatemala (ODHAG) and, just two days before his death, the seventy-five-year-old Gerardi had released a report entitled *Guatemala: Never Again*. The document, produced through the intensive work of a landmark Commission for the Recuperation of Historical Memory, confirmed what had long been suspected: that the overwhelming majority of massacres in the highlands during the early 1980s were the work of government forces.

At first an indigent man was arrested and later released for lack of evidence. Soon thereafter the investigation turned to another Catholic priest, Mario Orantes, who had served as Gerardi's assistant.

Unsatisfied, the ODHAG continued to pressure the government to pursue leads in the case, that seem to point to the involvement of the Guatemalan military. Other evidence has also come to light. Witnesses claim to have seen a pickup truck with military license plates parked in front of the church on the night of the murder. Other reports place a Mercedes Benz near the scene of the crime. The latter vehicle is registered to the military base at Chiquimula but is used by retired Colonel Byron Lima. Lima's son (Captain Byron Lima Olivia) was at the time a member of the elite Presidential Military Guard, with its headquarters not far from the San Sebastián Church.

These developments led President Arzú to make several announcements, promising a thorough investigation into the case. In one speech he even promised to order military officers to submit to DNA samples to determine if they were at the scene of the crime. However, three special prosecutors assigned to the case resigned, citing lack of cooperation from military and other government officials. One of these, who had ordered DNA samples from a small group of soldiers, fled the country in fear of his life. In addition, on April 16, 1999, unknown men broke into the home of Ronalth Ochaeta, the administrative director of the Archbishop's Human Rights Office. During a several-hour siege they terrorized Ochaeta's four-year-old son and his housekeeper, stole documents relating to the Gerardi case, and left a cardboard box with a large chunk of concrete in it, a reminder of what had happened to Gerardi and, by implication, the fate of others who investigate war crimes.

In July 1998, Ríos Montt's brother, a Catholic bishop, was appointed the Archdiocese Ombudsman for Human Rights, filling the position left vacant by Bishop Gerardi's assassination and making the irony complete. Claiming a firm division between family life and public duties, Monsignor Mario Ríos Montt does not feel that his brother's former position and current political interests will affect the way he does his job. And to his credit he pressed the government to resolve the Gerardi case.

The case finally came to trial in March 2001, with Colonel Bryon Lima, his son, Captain Byron Lima, Sergeant José Villanueva (also a member of the Presidential Guard), Orantes, and Margarita López (Gerardi's housekeeper) as defendants. The younger Byron Lima began the trial by shouting anti-communist slogans from the defense table. Finally, on June 8, a three-judge panel returned its verdict. The two Byron Limas and Villanueva were convicted of "extra-judicial execution" (a charge that implies state sponsorship) and sentenced to thirty years in prison each. Reverend Orantes was convicted as an accomplice and sentenced to a twenty-year prison term; López was acquitted. This was the first time in Guatemalan history that army officers had been convicted of a political crime, a watershed event in Guatemalan human rights. At the same time, it is widely assumed that the intellectual authors of the murder are to be found higher up in the army's chain of command. As of late 2001, a judicial committee continues to investigate the Gerardi murder, with the hopes of building cases against more army brass.

In other chapters of this book, we return to the impact of the violence on the central highlands, the recent as well as more distant history of the region, and what it means to be Maya child, farmer, or Kaqchikel speaker in Tecpán at the turn of the millennium. However, first we turn to the layers of histories that inform contemporary life in Tecpán.

Notes

1. The Gini index is notoriously difficult to calculate. Most data on wealth distribution, particularly from countries such as Guatemala, are fragmentary at best. Gini indices vary, giving Guatemala a score as high as .85 and as low as .508. Regardless of the precision of these rankings, it is clear even to the casual observer that Guatemala is a country of dramatic contrasts in wealth. Figures in the text are from the World Bank World Development Indicators, available at www.worldbank.org/data/wdi.

2. "I, Rigoberta Menchú, liar," *Salon* (1999), available at www.salon.com/col/horo/1999/01/nc_11horo2.html.

Further Reading

Carmack, Robert M., ed. 1988. *Harvest of violence: The Maya indians and the Guatemalan crisis.* Norman: University of Oklahoma Press.

Handy, Jim. 1984. *Gift of the devil: A history of Guatemala.* Toronto: Between the Lines.

Montejo, Victor. 1987. *Testimony: Death of a Guatemalan village.* Willimantic, CT: Curbstone Press.

Nelson, Diane M. 1999. *A finger in the wound: Body politics in quincentennial Guatemala.* Berkeley: University of California Press.

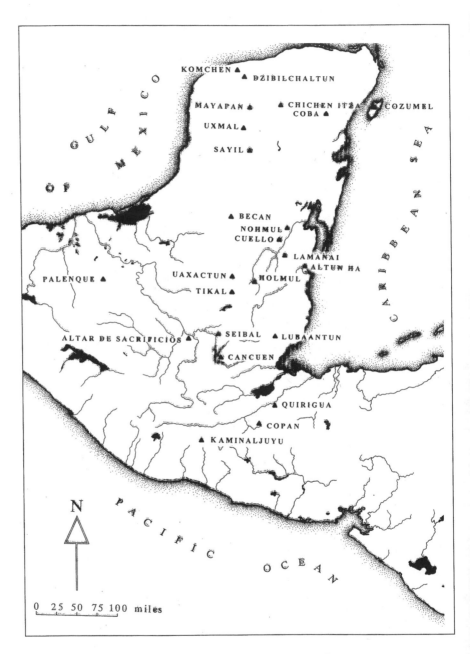

KOMCHEN ▲
▲ ĐZIBILCHALTUN

MAYAPAN ▲   ▲ CHICHEN ITZA ◁ COZUMEL
                      COBA ▲

UXMAL ▲

SAYIL ▲

▲ BECAN
NOHMUL ▲
CUELLO ▲
            ▲ LAMANAI
            ▲ ALTUN HA
UAXACTUN ▲
          ▲ HOLMUL
TIKAL ▲

PALENQUE ▲

ALTAR DE SACRIFICIOS ▲   ▲ SEIBAL   ▲ LUBAANTUN
                          ▲ CANCUEN

                          ▲ QUIRIGUA

                          ▲ COPAN

                  ▲ KAMINALJUYU

GULF OF MEXICO

CARIBBEAN SEA

N

PACIFIC OCEAN

0 25 50 75 100 miles

Ancient Maya cities. Courtesy of Arthur Demarest.

3

Maya Histories

For many foreigners, the notion of "Maya culture" brings to mind images of the pre-Columbian sites seen in *National Geographic* or public television documentaries: the meticulously constructed stone pyramids rising majestically out of the jungle canopy, the painstakingly carved stone monuments commemorating kings or sacrificial prisoners, the vividly colored murals depicting scenes of bloodletting and ceremonial debauchery. Such popular representations usually note that Maya culture is not dead, that millions of Maya people continue to live in Mexico, Guatemala, Belize, and Honduras. Yet in these portrayals the modern Maya are often simultaneously represented as the noble descendants of a once great civilization and the victims of encroaching modern progress—heroes and victims, the stuff of romantic musings.

The reality is much more complex. Maya today are not merely a group of people reacting to forces of modernization. They are a diverse population living in several different countries who are actively engaged in constructing their own future, using whatever resources are at hand to pursue their self-conceived best interests. And while the past weighs heavily on the present, the Maya are not slaves to history; elements of pre-Columbian ideologies remain strong today in Maya communities such as Tecpán, but they have become indelibly mixed with Western traditions to create new hybrid cultural forms that are considered "Maya." Many lament this change, romantically idealizing some pure past that has been corrupted and eroded by contact with the West. However, by their very nature all cultures are hybrids, constantly changing to adapt to new circumstances, and in this sense Maya culture is no different.

A few kilometers outside of Tecpán's urban center sits the archaeological site of Iximche', the pre-Columbian capital of the Kaqchikel empire (see Figure 3.1). Operated as a park by the national government, the area includes the reconstructed

Figure 3.1   Iximche', the capital of the Postclassic Kaqchikel kingdom, located outside of modern Tecpán.

temples, ball courts, and foundations of a number of pre-Conquest urban struc-tures; a museum, picnic area, and soccer field; and an active Maya sacred space on top of and surrounding a small unexcavated building at the far end of the site. Iximche' is a popular spot for locals and tourists to visit, and on weekends the park-ing lot is filled with cars and tour buses, and the grounds just outside the excava-tions are active with families eating picnic lunches, playing soccer, or checking out the crafts on sale. For many visitors, Iximche' is a convenient rest stop halfway be-tween Guatemala City and the resort areas of Lake Atitlán, and the time they spend in the archaeological site and museum is brief. For others, Iximche' is a place where they can learn about Maya history and get a "feel" for a city that was vibrant 500 years ago. Their visit is a destination point on an educational pilgrimage that might also include stops at Zaculeu, Tikal, Copán, and other ancient ruins.

However, for a growing number of Maya visitors—and for Kaqchikel Tecpanecos in particular—Iximche' is more than a relic of some distant past. It provides tangible evidence of what their ancestors made and where they lived hundreds of years ago and, in a more active sense, it also gives power and histori-cal force to current projects. Thus, in recent years Tecpán's Indian fair queens have gone to Iximche' as part of their investiture. Escorted by the town's *ladino* queens and Indian queens invited from other towns, the two indigenous Tecpán queens are the subjects of a religious ceremony on the ancient site. In the past, all

Figure 3.2 The fountain in the park facing the Catholic church. Note the Classic Maya motifs.

the public activities of being queen took place in the town center. Now, in an era being referred to by some as a Maya renaissance, their appearances at dances and parades in the "new" town are given more historical force because of these confirming activities at Iximche'. The term "heritage tourism" is used to label the phenomenon of people making tourist pilgrimages to sites that are important to them by virtue of ties to their family, town, or nation. Recent writings on some of these places critically examine how the sites (and memories) are constructed and understood by visitors (see, for example, Handler and Gable 1997 on Colonial Williamsburg and Kirshenblatt-Gimblett 1998 on a number of sites worldwide).

The present is constructed—consciously or unconsciously—from historical experience, both the material conditions produced by past actions and the remembrance of how things once were. Thus, to understand the lives of contemporary Maya it is important to understand their history. Ideas of what is acceptable and appropriate are internalized from past experience and custom, and in this way history makes its mark on the present. This is not a new idea; in *The 18th Brumaire of Louis Bonaparte* (1852), Karl Marx notes that:

Men make their own history, but they do not make it just as they please;
they do not make it under circumstances chosen by themselves, but under
circumstances directly encountered, given, and transmitted from the past.
The tradition of all the dead generations weighs like a nightmare on the
brain of the living. And just when they seem engaged in revolutionizing
themselves and things, in creating something that has never yet existed,
precisely in such periods of revolutionary crisis they anxiously conjure up
the spirits of the past to their service and borrow from them names, battle
cries, and costumes in order to present the new scene of world history in
this time-honored disguise and this borrowed language.

And so it is with the Maya of Tecpán as well: The present is filtered through an understanding of the past, and even novel actions implicitly reference shared notions of a common history.

That said, it is important to realize that people are intentional and active actors working toward their own (individual and collective) self-interests. History may be seen as sequences of events that build upon each other; however, their direction is not predetermined but rather formed in the heat of practice. Maya culture has not developed in isolation, nor has it evolved following a predetermined path. Rather the Maya present is an accumulation of events over time, junctures with larger systems (the Spanish Conquest, the globalization of the Information Age), and the actions of intentional cultural actors.

REACHING BACK TO THE LIVES OF THE ANCIENT MAYA

The *Popol Vuh* is an early colonial manuscript written in the K'iche' Mayan language using Latin characters. It was written by K'iche' elite as a means of controlling and representing their own history to make claims on the Spanish colonial administration. A creation story, the *Popol Vuh* highlights the covenantal relationship between humans (the K'iche' lords, in particular) and their creators. The scribes who wrote the *Popol Vuh* describe three initial creations in which the gods try unsuccessfully to create beings who would praise them and offer sacrifices as their part of a reciprocal relationship that would maintain cosmic balance and perpetuate the cycle of existence. At first, the gods created the plants and animals, but the animals could not praise their creators and so were killed and eaten. Next, a person was created from mud; however, not only was it unable to speak properly, it dissolved before it could multiply. Then people were made of wood and they multiplied, but they lacked hearts and minds and were met by multiple destructions: They were gouged, torn open, and washed away by a great flood. Their descendants live on as howler monkeys. At this point in the *Popol Vuh* the narrative of the creation is seemingly interrupted by a series of adventures of the twin gods, Hunahpu and Xbalanque, whose father and uncle have been defeated on the ball court in Xibalba, the underworld. After the twin gods defeat the lords of Xibalba and reestablish order in the cosmos by satisfying a number of challenges (challenges that could be construed as having to do with the very things that human lords will have to master), the creation story continues. With the fourth attempt, humans are successfully created from corn and water and charged with maintaining the sacred covenant through tribute, sacrifice, and praise. The K'iche' lords in particular succeed in honoring the gods and also ruling the earth.

Although the *Popol Vuh* was written in manuscript form around 1550, scenes from this mythistory (Tedlock 1985) also appear on pottery and monuments found throughout the Maya region that date to hundreds of years before the Conquest (Coe 1992). These attest to both the centrality and longevity of rites such as blood sacrifice in Maya societies. During the Classic Era, what might be seen as the "height" of Maya civilization, it appears that blood sacrifice was the most valued form of offering, and stelae record the painful rituals of running a thorned vine through the tongue or perforating the penis with a stingray spine. Today, for the families who continue to practice Maya religion, it is common to burn incense; offer liquor, sugar, chocolate, and perfumes; and perhaps kill a chicken or goat. In some families it is also customary to offer verbal supplication before harvesting crops or cutting down a tree. Despite the dramatically different contexts in which these rites have been practiced, certain central elements of the sacred Mesoamerican covenant emerge: the notions of debt and reciprocity, of fate that can be influenced by one's actions, and of obedience to authority. (See Monaghan 1995 for a similar belief system among the Mixtecs of Oaxaca, Mexico.)

This covenant blessed Maya rulers in the Classic Period (circa AD 250–900), allowing them to build up impressive city-states such as Tikal, Copán, and Palenque. (Tikal, one of the larger sites, is estimated to have had an urban population of about 10,000, with another 30,000 living nearby—comparable in size to modern Tecpán.) The Classic Maya developed complex calendars and a hieroglyphic writing system; intensive agricultural techniques to provision their large urban centers; and a stratified sociopolitical system to coordinate trade, tribute, and warfare. These were civilizations, however, carved out of a precarious natural environment, the tropical lowland forests of present-day Guatemala, Mexico, Belize, and Honduras. By the ninth century AD the system was overextended. It seems likely that environmental degradation played at least some role in weakening Maya cities, which required ever greater agricultural production to supply growing populations. Environmental strains led to political tensions, and hieroglyphic texts record increasingly intense wars between city-states. As a result, Classic Maya civilization "collapsed" during the early tenth century, with cities largely abandoned; the construction of monumental architecture ceased; and writing was no longer practiced.

Before even considering the Maya idea of temporality, it bears mentioning that the notion of time is a cultural construct, even if our own notions of time often seem to be naturally given. The ways in which time is conceived vary greatly

Archaeological Sequence for the Maya Area

Humans first reached the New World via the Bering Strait as early as 50,000 years ago or as recently as 12,000 years ago, depending on how one interprets certain Carbon–14 dates and a few controversial early archaeological sites in Brazil and Chile. These first Americans were nomadic foragers and hunters of mammoth and buffalo, images deduced from the few stone tools (difficult at first glance to distinguish from broken rocks) and butchered animal carcasses that remain. Archaeologists term this the "Paleo-Indian Period" and classify other periods as follows:

25,000 YA–7000 BC	Paleo-Indian Period
7000–2300 BC	Archaic Period
2300 BC–AD 250	Pre-Classic (or Formative) Period
AD 250–900	Classic Maya Period
AD 900–contact	Postclassic Maya Period

Such chronological schemes are helpful in discussing broad trends in the archaeological record, and they are based on real material data. The Archaic Period is marked by a shift toward hunting smaller animals (deer, rabbits) and a greater reliance on wild fruits, nuts, and vegetables; the tool kit used by Archaic-era peoples becomes streamlined and more refined, reflecting changing uses. In the Pre-Classic Period, domestic agriculture begins to take hold, leading to sedentary village life; this is recorded in the archaeological record by the emergence of clay pottery (too cumbersome for nomadic peoples), year-round occupation of a single site (with more permanent structures, and the post-holes that they leave behind), and pronounced social stratification (seen in settlement patterns, architectural styles, and the manufacture and trade of luxury goods). As its moniker suggests, the Pre-Classic Period is seen as a prelude to the Classic Maya era, during which lowland city-states grew dramatically in wealth and power, grand temples and palaces were constructed, and the arts and sciences (writing, mathematics, astronomy) were highly developed. In this progression, the Post-Classic Period is often portrayed as a denouement to Classic era glories: The great cities were largely abandoned, the art of hieroglyphic writing appears to have been lost, and the locus of development shifted from lowland polities to emergent highland Maya kingdoms. The expansion of highland kingdoms, particularly the
(continued)

Archaeological Sequence for the Maya Area

(continued from page 48) Kaqchikeles based around Tecpán, came to a halt with the Spanish invasion in 1524.

Despite the utility of such chronological schemes, they should be treated with a healthy dose of skepticism because of the important aspects of cultural development that they hide. Most apparently, they offer a misleading precision in dating large-scale cultural shifts, changes that are exceedingly gradual and unevenly distributed throughout the Americas. Furthermore, Mesoamerican chronologies are very Classic Maya-centric: They impute a post hoc directionality to cultural change in which *Archaic* and *Pre-Classic* societies are seen to inevitably lead to the heights of *Classic* Maya *civilization* (note even the terminology used here). Such views hide the indeterminacy of cultural change in practice, the competing intentions and actions of cultural actors, and the diversity of cultural responses (admittedly, all things that are hard to get at through the archaeological record). They also unwittingly play into ethnocentric perspectives that see in modern Maya cultures only the degenerated remains of past glories.

from culture to culture. We in the West fetishize time, checking our watches, organizing our time precisely, and planning our classes and recreational schedules. This view of time is markedly progressive, which is to say that it is most often viewed in a linear fashion: times change, the present is built on the past, and the future stretches ahead of us. From such a perspective it is easy to assume a given direction to historical change: progress.

For the ancient Maya, time and history also held special importance, but different from our own notions. The Classic Maya viewed time as fundamentally cyclic rather than as a simple linear progression. They employed elaborate calendars, based on increasingly large cycles of time, and it appears that they either wrote their histories to conform to calendrical cyclicity, or they arranged historically important events to coincide with meaningful calendrical dates. Most likely both strategies were used. As Barbara Tedlock (1982) points out, the Maya were not drones reenacting a strict cyclical history; rather they viewed the passing of time as accumulative. She writes that "the burdens of time do not so much change as accumulate" (1982: 202), and these cyclic accumulations can give birth to new structures and beliefs.

The Classic Maya employed several different calendrical systems simultaneously, one of which is still used today by Tecpaneco "day-keepers." Studying Maya calendars, one must first understand that the Maya numeration is vigesimal (a base-twenty system, as opposed to our base-ten, or decimal, system). This means basically that numbers are counted in groups of twenty. In Classic Maya mathematics, groups of twenty were represented by a hierarchical system of positional symbols; numerical modifiers for these groups (numbers less than 20) were represented by bars (which equal "5") and dots (which equal "1"). Thus, a single bar topped by one dot equaled "6"; likewise, three bars underneath three dots equaled "18" (see Figure 3.3).

Figure 3.3   Maya bar and dot notations representing 0, 6, and 18.

Classic Maya mathematics served important scientific, religious, and political functions. Amazingly precise astronomical tables were produced, allowing scholars and priests to make exact predictions of eclipses and planetary movements; a complex system of numerological divinations was developed, giving scientific exactitude to religious beliefs; and political leaders deftly deployed such mathematical knowledge in political rhetoric, which served to solidify their power.

Believing that there are important cycles in the progression of history, calendars were of particular importance to the Classic Maya. The Long Count calendar records absolute dates, and its widespread use on stone stelae has preserved for us a detailed historical record of dynastic lineages and regional warfare throughout the Classic Maya era. The Long Count records elapsed time from a conventional starting point, just as our own contemporary, Gregorian, calendar does. Whereas our calendar uses the purported year of Jesus's birth as a starting point (1 January, AD 1), the Maya Long Count began on the date written as 13.0.0.0.0 4 Ahau 8 Kumk'u (which is either the eleventh or thirteenth of August 3114 BCE in the Gregorian calendar, depending on what correlation one uses). The first five digits of this date are the Long Count, showing 13 Bak'tuns, 0 K'atuns, 0 Tuns, 0 Winals, and 0 K'ins; a k'in is one day, a winal is twenty k'ins, a tun is composed of 18 winals or 360 days (breaking the vigesimal order somewhat to better approximate the solar year), a k'atun is 20 tuns (7,200 days, about 19.7 years), and a

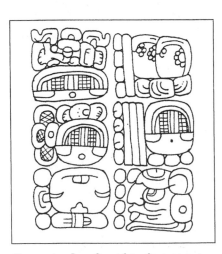

Figure 3.4   Long Count date of 9.0.19.2.4, or 14 October AD 454 (1,302,884 days since 11 August 3114 BCE).

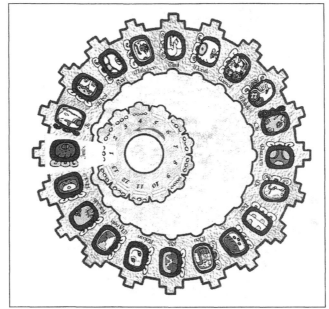

*Figure 3.5
Representation of the
Classic Maya Calendar
Round. Reproduced by
permission from Sidney
Hollander from
Calendario Maya and
its website at www.cal–
endariomaya.com.*

bak'tun is 20 k'atuns (144,000 days, or about 394 years). Figure 3.4 shows a typical Long Count date as found on a Maya stelae.

Also important, especially for divination, was the fifty-two-year Calendar Round, the two dates following the Long Count. The Calendar Round consisted of two related calendrical cycles, not unlike our days of the week and months of the year. The first was the *haab*, made up of eighteen months of twenty days followed by an especially unlucky period of five days: a 365-day solar year. (It bears mention that the Classic Maya calendar was more accurate than the Julian calendar then employed in the Western world; only in 1582, when Pope Gregory XIII ordered ten days dropped from October and established our current Gregorian system with leap years, did the Christian calendar obtain a more precise measure.) In the *haab*, a numerical coefficient rotates from 1 to 20, modifying a named month (e.g., 8 Kumk'u is followed by 9 Kumk'u) which will change after twenty days. The *haab* is further correlated to another calendar, called by archaeologists and epigraphers the *tzolkin*. The *tzolkin* is a 260-day calendar made up of thirteen numerical coefficients and twenty named days (e.g., Ahau, Ixim, Oq); in the *tzolkin* cycle both the day name and its numerical coefficient change each day (thus 1 Ahau is followed by 2 Ixix, which is followed by 3 Ik'). Figure 3.5 illustrates the Calendar Round's movement.

The *tzolkin*, or *chol q'ij* in Kaqchikel, is still used by traditional Maya day-keepers (*aj q'ijaj*, sing. *aj q'ij*) working in Tecpán, and they have elaborate mnemonic systems to help them remember the days and their divinational significance. What is more, modern Maya scholars and activists as well as foreign scholars of

Figure 3.6   Maya priest drawing day name in sugar as part of a ceremonial offering. Ted records the prayers for transcription later.

the Maya have been working to resurrect and revitalize Maya calendars and hieroglyphic writing for many years. The late epigrapher Linda Schele ran an annual workshop for Maya participants on how to read the glyphs, and the syllabaries she handed out have been widely reproduced and circulated in Maya communities (for more on Maya revitalization see Fischer and Brown 1996; for further resources on Maya glyphs visit our website, which includes links to calculators that allow you to convert any Gregorian date into a Maya date).

POSTCLASSIC HIGHLANDS

In the centuries between the Classic Maya collapse and the arrival of Spaniards, a number of Maya polities arose in the highland regions of western Guatemala and southern Mexico. Prominent among these was the Kaqchikel kingdom. The history of the Kaqchikeles is one of warfare and intrigue, tenuous relations with their neighbors, and strategic alliances with other groups including, eventually, the Spaniards. Our knowledge of the period is incomplete, gleaned from disparate sources written both by native Kaqchikeles and the Spanish conquerors. Hieroglyphic writing never seems to have reached into the highlands, so we do not have the rich documentary evidence that has shed so much light on Classic lowland Maya civilization. By popular architectural standards, the highland Maya centers were also less spectacular than their lowland counterparts, and thus have not attracted the archaeological attention of the more famous lowland sites.[1]

Linguistically, politically, and historically, the Kaqchikeles are related to the K'iche' and only separated from the K'iche' polity around 1,000 years ago. In the twelfth century, according to the dates worked out by Robert Carmack (1981), the K'iche'an peoples entered the highland areas that are today western Guatemala. They established a capital city at the site known as Utatlán. By the early fifteenth century, the K'iche' had undertaken a massive project of political expansion, backed up by their formidable military power. Both Kaqchikel and K'iche' documents report that an important part of the K'iche' military might was attributable to the Kaqchikeles, who were closely aligned with the K'iche'. It appears that this alignment happened because the K'iche' were able to leverage their prestige and superior political organization to induce the Kaqchikeles to serve them, working them into their system of ranked lineages as "junior brothers."

The Kaqchikeles also acted as their warriors or mercenaries and were much valued by K'iche' rulers for their battlefield adeptness. Several important K'iche' victories are directly attributed to Kaqchikel forces, and Carmack (1981) suggests that the name "Kaqchikel," which may be glossed as "red stick people," refers to a symbol of warfare.

The best single source of precontact history among the Kaqchikeles is the manuscript known as the *Anales of the Kaqchikeles*. Probably originally written in the late sixteenth century, it survives today as a copy made in the seventeenth century and now housed in the library of the University of Pennsylvania. The document is of special interest to Kaqchikel Maya scholars and activists, who see it as an almost scared social charter. In 1998, Ted accompanied a group of Kaqchikeles to Philadelphia to examine the manuscript. After filling out the proper paperwork and donning archival gloves, the group gathered around a table to gaze upon the perfectly preserved handwritten text. The emotion was palpable as pages were reverently turned and favored passages read aloud. Much more than an intellectual enterprise, the scene was reminiscent of family members seeing documents signed by ancestors on Ellis Island or an ancestral tome from the old country.

The *Anales*, like other surviving native colonial texts, is written in a genre rich in poetry and word play as well as historical description. The following passages come from a transcription and translation of the *Anales of the Kaqchikeles* done by the Oxlajuuj Keej Maya' Ajtz'iib' (13 Deer Maya Writers), a group of native Maya linguists. Like many Mesoamerican histories, the *Anales* offer an account of Kaqchikel origins in terms of successive migrations. It is said that they traveled over water: "From the west we came to Tulán, from across the sea . . . and after the seven tribes had arrived, we the warriors came. So they said. And commanding us to come , they said to us, our mothers, our fathers: 'Go my daughters, my sons. I will give you your wealth, your domain; I will give you your power and your majesty, your canopy and your throne.'" Likewise, each migration was spurred on by the will of the gods and their promises of riches and wealth awaiting them, and of land to call their own:

Kecha' ri e ojer qatata' qamama'	So said our ancient parents and grandparents:
Oj juwi chi ajlab'al	We are a group of warriors
xa ruma ri nim kipus kinawal	because we have a great magic power
je na wi pe je iqayom ri ch'a' pokob'	they are the ones that carry the spears and shields
ke re' k'a xelajib'ex wi kiwach,	and in this way they paid homage
e nab'ey qamama' ri'	to our first grandparents
ruma ri k'iy xuqasaj ruq'ij ralaxik.	who had brought together many.

The *Anales* provide long lists of the towns and areas that the Kaqchikeles conquered while aligned with the K'iche'. Backed by Kaqchikel fighting power, the K'iche's rapidly became the most powerful group in the highland region. Particularly during the rule of Kiq'ab (circa 1425–1475) the K'iche's expanded their domain with the help of Kaqchikel warriors, thereby enlarging the area from which tribute was collected. It is unclear just where the Kaqchikeles lived during this period of K'iche' expansion, but Fox (1978) and Carmack (1981) suggest that the site of Pakaman, located two kilometers southeast of Utatlán, was their home base, and it seems likely that as warriors the Kaqchikeles were probably stationed at other sites throughout the K'iche' heartland as well. They retained a distinct language and view of themselves as a group during this period, however, and were never wholly integrated into K'iche' society. Under the rule of Kiq'ab the Kaqchikeles built and occupied a new town on the eastern border of the K'iche' empire, a place named Chiawar Tz'upitak'aj ("Fortified Plains of Milpa," as Carmack translates it), and from this base expanded the K'iche' empire eastward. But by 1470, Kiq'ab's rapid expansion was beginning to take its toll on the K'iche' empire, and his power was being contested by subordinates. The *Anales* tell that one day a K'iche' warrior demanded that a Kaqchikel market woman give him a piece of produce. The woman refused, and Kiq'ab ordered the soldier arrested for molesting the woman, but his warriors resisted, demanding instead that the woman be turned over to the authorities. To avert a slaughter of the Kaqchikeles, the embattled Kiq'ab traveled furtively one night to the Kaqchikel city. There he thanked the Kaqchikeles for their service to him but warned that he could no longer hold back his warriors, and urged them ("my children") to flee.

Flee they did, to the south, where they established a new capital city, Iximche', embarking upon their own program of military expansion. Meanwhile, K'iche' warriors made several attempts to reconquer the Kaqchikeles after the split, but they were never successful. On the eve of Spanish arrival, the Kaqchikeles were clearly the ascendant polity in the highlands as the K'iche' empire contracted (See Figure 3.7.).

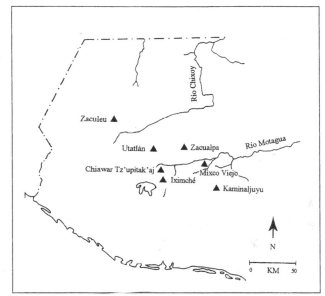

Figure 3.7　Important sites in the Postclassic Maya highlands.

The Kaqchikel capital at Iximche' must have been an amazing sight in its heyday. Stone plazas were circled by whitewashed temples, and palaces were topped with thatched roof shelters. The site is surrounded by deep *barrancos* (canyons) carved into the landscape by ancient earthquakes and erosion. Precipitous slopes on three sides make it virtually impossible to reach the site except by means of the one level entrance, which was protected by fortifications. Outposts located on hilltops around the site provided a clear view of the surrounding region, from Lake Atitlán to Comalapa. Such fortifications were necessary given the tense political relations between highland Maya groups in the fifteenth century. Carmack estimates the Iximche' population at 10,000, about the same as modern-day Tecpán.

The Kaqchikel kingdom was ruled by four leaders, each of whom was represented in the city's layout with his own plaza. Even today Tecpán is divided into four barrios, perhaps an allusion to the previous quadripartite system. The Kaqchikel empire based at Iximche' suffered its own internal revolt. In 1493 the Tukuche' lineage left Iximche' and established its own capital to the east at a site known as Mixco Viejo, around what is today the town of San Martín Jilotepeque. There they bordered on the territory of a third Kaqchikel polity, the Akajal (or Chajomá).

In 1524, Pedro de Alvarado, one of Cortés' lieutenants in the conquest of Mexico, set forth to conquer the Maya peoples to the south. The Spaniards had heard reports of great Maya wealth; one can imagine the Aztecs eagerly pointing the Spanish soldiers southward, appealing to their endless thirst for gold. Sent with Cortés' blessing, Alvarado traveled with 120 horsemen, 300 foot soldiers, a few small artillery pieces, and several hundred native Mexican troops (Tlaxcalans)

(Hill 1992: 19). In February 1524 Alvarado and his troops reached Utatlán, seat of the K'iche' kingdom. The formal arrival of the Spaniards had been preceded by several years by the arrival of Spanish diseases, the first shock wave of the Conquest (see Lovell and Cook 1991; Lovell 1992).

When Alvarado arrived, Iximche' had a dual ruler system, led by the kings Kaji' Imox and Belehe Qat. The Kaqchikel rulers initially aligned themselves with the Spaniards and sent a reported 2,000 troops to help them defeat the K'iche'. Likely it was thought that by aligning with this new powerful political force they could expand their domination over the highland region and crush their enemies. Although it is easy to forget now, the Kaqchikeles at the time did not know how long the Spaniards would stay or how regional political systems were to be forever upset by long-term Spanish colonization. After Alvarado's arrival at Iximche', Kaqchikel leaders were consulted about their other enemies in the area—the Tz'utujil to the west and the Pipil community to the southwest, in present-day El Salvador—and the Spaniards along with their Mexican and Kaqchikel allied troops quickly conquered these small kingdoms. But Alvarado and his men returned to Iximche' from these conquests unsatisfied, their thirst for gold and riches unquenched. And on July 25, 1524, Alvarado and his men established Guatemala's first Spanish capital (Tecpán Guatemala) at Iximche'. Spanish demands rapidly increased, and many Kaqchikeles, including nobles, were forced to pan for gold. By September 1524, less than five months after Alvarado first arrived, the Kaqchikeles decided that they could take no more of the cruel *conquistador* demands and they revolted, large numbers fleeing to the forests, where they would stay in exile for over three years. In May 1540, years after the Spanish moved their capital city away from Tecpán, Alvarado ordered the last Kaqchikel king hanged to stem any further attempts at rebellion.

SPANISH COLONIZATION

Spanish colonization exacted dramatic changes in Kaqchikel lifeways. Colonial life was rife with exploitation, and archival documents from the period record a steady stream of Indian complaints over forced labor, excessive tribute demands, and fraudulent land claims. In the absence of large gold and silver deposits, Maya people were Guatemala's most valuable resource and became victims of the colonial system, with many forced to provide unpaid labor and suffer declining living conditions plus the loss of their lands.

During the colonial period the Maya were subject to many different forms of labor tribute. Under the early *encomienda* system, Spaniards were given the right to labor and tribute in kind from Indian populations occupying a given plot of land. These grants were intended both to reward the roles that the *conquistadors* played in the pacification and to provide a means for developing the rural economy of the colony (and thus to collect tribute). Very soon, however, the Spanish Crown began to worry about the excessive power wielded by *encomenderos* and,

Iximche' Chronology

1470–1490	Kaqchikel spilt from K'iche'; Iximche' established.
1490	K'iche' attempt to reconquer the Kaqchikeles; defeated.
1493	Tukuche' revolt at Iximche'.
1510	Montezuma's messengers arrive to warn of Spaniards' arrival.
1513	Fire at Iximche'; site rebuilt.
1515–1518	More wars with the K'iche'; Kaqchikeles consistently victorious.
1521	Smallpox epidemic at Iximche'.
12 April 1524	Alvarado conquers Utatlán.
14 April 1524	Alvarado arrives at Iximche' and soon after leaves for El Salvador.
25 July 1524	Alvarado returns to Iximche' and founds a Spanish *villa* there.
5 September 1524	Kaqchikeles revolt against Spaniards.
22 November 1527	Spanish capital moved to Almolonga.
12 January 1528	Kaqchikeles again start paying Spanish tribute.
26 May 1540	Alvarado hangs the Kaqchikel leader Kaji' Imox.

(SOURCE: Adapted from Borg [1980].)

in 1542, a set of "New Laws" was enacted to govern colonial relations. The *repartimiento* system tried to temper the potential for abuses by inserting a Spanish official between Spanish landlords and Indian subjects, with limited success.

Most accounts of the Spanish colonial period in Guatemala rightly stress the exploitation suffered by the Maya peoples as an important part of the Maya experience. Yet it is easy to oversimplify and see the Maya as mere victims in the historical process—fighting in vain to hold onto their traditional culture in the face of increasing hispanization of society, struggling under the yoke of tribute burdens while trying to maintain their traditional system of subsistence agriculture. This perspective, however, loses sight of the Maya as active and intentional actors in their own history. The following examples demonstrate how Maya peoples from Tecpán actively engaged the new Spanish system of governance and economics.

The Xpantzay Lawsuit
The dark and dusty General Archive of Central America, located in downtown Guatemala City, houses shelf upon shelf of colonial documents, testament to the Spanish propensity for legal documentation. Call number A5 3957 6062

brings up the paperwork of a 1658 lawsuit by Indians from Tecpán against two Creole landowners.[2]

The story begins in 1569, when one of the first *conquistadors* of Guatemala, a man named Alonso Gutiérrez de Monzón, was given a royal grant of a large tract of land lying between the town centers of Tecpán, Patzún, and Patzicía. Revealing the Crown's at least nominal commitment to protecting the Indians entrusted to its care, the grant was predicated on the condition that no herds of cows, bulls, or horses (*ganado mayor*) were to be established on the land, lest they threaten adjacent Indian crops. By the mid-seventeenth century the land in question had been passed down over several generations and transferred between families at least once. Eventually the land was inherited by Francisco de Argueta, who, along with an associate, proceeded to place several large herds of cattle on the land. In 1658 Pedro López Xpantzay led a group of kinsmen and other Indians from Tecpán in suing Argueta for return of the land based on Argueta's violation of the terms of the original grant.

Xpantzay retained a Spanish legal advocate and in 1658 submitted to the court a set of Kaqchikel documents now known as the "Títulos de los Xpantzay." As is common in such colonial petitions, the Xpantzay documents begin by tracing the history of the Kaqchikel people from long before the arrival of the Spaniards. They recount a migration to Tula and then to the highlands, the conquest of the highlands at the side of the K'iche', and the split from the K'iche' and the establishment of Iximche'. Using native place names to mark boundaries, the Xpantzay documents also record the extent of lands controlled by them and other native families before the Conquest. The Xpantzay lawsuit presents these testaments as evidence in the action against Argueta, dramatically calling for a huge parcel of ancestral lands to be repatriated to the community.

Legal proceedings lasted for five years, until, in 1663, the Xpantzay won a final ruling in their suit against Argueta. Figure 3.8 shows the area that the court mandated be returned to the Indians. That the Indian plaintiffs won runs counter to simplistic representations of colonial oppression and shows the willingness and capability of Tecpaneco Indians to work within the Spanish legal tradition to fight for their own self-advancement (see also Hill 1989: 179–187).

Guigui Dispute

By the turn of the nineteenth century the Spanish empire was in its waning days. Resistance to the highly centralized system of economic and political control was growing, and Indians in Tecpán continued to press for their interests in the Spanish legal system. One example comes from an 1807–1808 dispute between Tecpán's Indian governor and the Spanish Corregidor of Chimaltenango, or the head of the regional administrative department.

During the colonial period, Tecpán was legally classified as a *pueblo indio* (an Indian town), a designation that severely limited the rights of Spaniards living there. Notably, most local government was placed in the hands of nominally

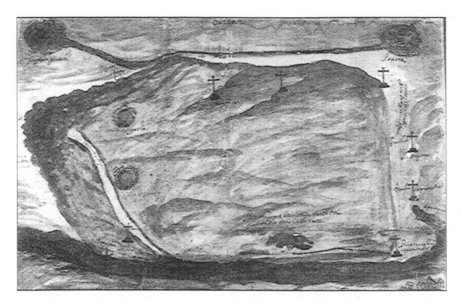

Figure 3.8   Seventeenth-century map of lands around Tecpán returned to Indian plaintiffs in the Xpantzay lawsuit. Tecpán ("Tecpanguatemala") is in the upper left corner.

elected Indian officials, led by an Indian governor. For the most part, the colonial administration was content to collect adequate tribute and left the particulars of day to day management to the local government. Pueblos such as Tecpán were part of larger administrative units know as *corregimientos*; for example, Tecpán was under the control of the Corregidor of Chimaltenango. The regional Spanish authorities of *corregidores* were, in turn, answerable to the Audiencia of Guatemala.

In 1807 the Corregidor of Chimaltenango, Don José del Barrio, who had confirmed the last several elections in Tecpán in which Felipe Guigui was elected the Indian governor, left office for reasons unrecorded in the documentary record. He was replaced by an interim Corregidor, Don Antonio Arrivillaga, who had had a long history of personal disputes against Guigui. Taking advantage of the opportunity afforded by his new position, Arrivillaga set out to remove Guigui from his position in Tecpán. Arrivillaga likely thought his position was unassailable: He was Spanish, he held an office that allowed almost absolute power in his jurisdiction, and almost all governors were guilty of some misdeeds. He was proven wrong.

On 22 November 1807 Arrivillaga traveled to Tecpán and held a surprise election in which a new Indian governor was elected. Election documents record that Guigui was present for the election, as was his right. In documents submitted to the Audiencia, the highest Spanish authority in Guatemala, Guigui supplied evidence that he was in fact not present for the election and asked that the results be nullified. Meanwhile, Arrivillaga returned to Tecpán and initiated an investigation into the finances of Guigui's administration. In a document dated 7 December 1807, several respected community leaders signed a deposition declaring that some 321 pesos had been misused from the municipal coffers and implicating Guigui in their disappearance.

On 21 January 1808, the president of the Audiencia of Guatemala, Don Antonio Gonzales Mollinedo y Saravin, issued a scathing ruling against Arrivillaga in the Guigui affair. In his formal decree, he writes that:

> *There is ample evidence that the interim Corregidor sees in the person of the Indian governor a mortal enemy and a witness quick to always denounce his conduct in administering repartimientos [Spanish labor tributes]; and he has made of this misfortune a victim of his resentments and vengeance, one to whom is due the protection of the Fiscal Minister, the common defender of the naturales [Indians], whose role is to maintain the rights of these miserable and oppressed peoples and raise them to the level which they desire.*
>
> *The acrid and venomous expressions produced by the interim Corregidor in his official capacity on 9 December [1807] condemning the conduct of the Indian governor and the results of the verbal judicial depositions obtained in the residence of Señor Averon concerning the election in Tecpanguatemala are unequivocal proof of the hatred and resentment with which Don Antonio Arrivillaga views Guigui.*
>
> *Recognizing that these naturales conducted a new election for the position of First Alcalde, with Guigui being reelected to continue in the office of Indian Governor, as attested to by the letter from Father Priest Don Francisco de Santo Banco on page 17 of this document ... it is decided that the Corregidor Arrivillaga, who acting on his own and suspending all pretexts, investigated the accounting irregularities that should be the providence of an ordinary Judge, and who never had the authority to fire the Indian governor as he did, much less given his position as an interim Corregidor.*

The tone of the Audiencia president's report is surprising. He obviously sees the Corregidor's behavior as reprehensible, but the Corregidor was also a Spaniard and probably expected to be treated with greater deference (most likely with a wink, a nudge, and a favorable ruling). That the report so severely condemns the Corregidor points to the fact that even though the odds were stacked against Indian plaintiffs, they did sometimes find justice within the Spanish system.

MAYA AGENCY AND THE COLONIAL ENCOUNTER

The Xpantzay lawsuit, the Guigui controversy, and a few other cases that remain in the archival record paint a clear picture of proactive native engagement with the Spanish system. Despite the many hardships that it involved, the Maya were able to coopt certain aspects of Spanish colonialism and use them toward their own ends—they were much more intentional agents than passive victims. Victoria Bricker (1981) makes a similar case in *The Indian Christ, The Indian King*, in which she shows how the Maya not only accommodated Spanish religious and political intrusions but used certain aspects of the Spanish beliefs to support and enrich their own long-established traditions.

All cultures are constantly in a state of flux; they are not homogeneous, static entities. At times, however, the pace of change may be accelerated. Such was the case in the Maya area after the Spanish invasion. Colonization dramatically shook up precontact Maya lifeways, changing everything from religious practice and settlement patterns to economic and political structures. But Maya culture (as lived by Maya individuals) was not helpless in the face of the formidable Spanish colonial machine. In both public performance and private belief, the Maya integrated Spanish mandates with local belief systems, creating a more cosmopolitan and hybrid Maya culture. And this process continues still, as the Maya adapt and redefine their culture in the face of an ever-changing post-colonial political system and an increasingly invasive world market system—all the while retaining a subjective sense of their culture's continuity.

Notes

1. One exception is the intensive interdisciplinary archaeological, historical, and ethnographic fieldwork conducted in the K'iche' area by Robert Carmack and his colleagues.
2. During the colonial period, there was an elaborate system of racial classification based on links to Spain. In this framework, Creoles were Spaniards born in the New World.

Further Reading

Demarest, Arthur. 2003. *Ancient Maya: The rise and fall of a rainforest civilization.* Cambridge: Cambridge University Press.

Freidel, David. A., Linda Schele, and Joy Parker. 1993. *Maya cosmos: Three thousand years on the shaman's path.* New York: William Morrow.

Hill, Robert M. 1992. *Colonial Cakchiquels: Highland Maya adaptations to Spanish rule, 1600–1700.* Fort Worth, TX: Harcourt Brace Jovanovich.

Soldiers from the local army base patrolling the street in Tecpán.

4

Natural Disaster, Political Violence, and Cultural Resurgence

In the predawn hours of February 4, 1976, Tecpanecos were woken by a violent earthquake that shook the entire highland region, registering 7.5 on the Richter scale. In Guatemala City several large buildings crumbled, and most of the old churches in the colonial city of Antigua were damaged, but in Tecpán the devastation was total. Official reports record the damage levels at 100 percent, and local residents confirm that nearly every building in town was destroyed. People say that one had to gain one's orientation by looking at the church facade, one of the only structures left partly standing.

The earthquake struck just after 3:00 A.M., perhaps the worst time possible because virtually everyone in town was at home in bed, and most of those who were killed were crushed by the clay tile roofs and adobe walls falling down. An estimated 3,000 people died in Tecpán, and the bodies were buried in mass graves dug by donated bulldozers. The parish priest at the time of the quake—by 1994 a frail, elderly man stationed in another town—recalled with tears in his eyes the last rites he performed over the pits filled with bodies. Visiting the Tecpán cemetery today, one is overwhelmed by the sea of gravestones bearing the date 4 February 1976 (see Figure 4.1).

Earthquakes and volcanic eruptions are not uncommon in the Guatemalan highlands, a geologically active region that is part of the tectonic border zone known as the Ring of Fire encircling the Pacific Ocean. The *Anales of the Kaqchikeles* record an earthquake so strong that it halted a war between the Kaqchikeles and a neighboring group. Earthquakes in 1773 devastated the then-capital city of Santiago (today's Antigua Guatemala), which led to the establishment of a new capital

Figure 4.1   Tecpán's cemetery, with headstone dated 4 February 1976.

city, Guatemala City. And tremendous quakes in late 1917 and early 1918 leveled most of Guatemala City and surrounding communities. However, the 1976 earthquake was by far the worst in recent history, killing some 23,000 people and injuring more than 76,000, mostly in the central highland region that includes Tecpán.

A number of Tecpanecos remember that on the day before the earthquake a pack of wolves appeared in town in the middle of the day, which in retrospect was an ominous sign. This story plays on salient distinctions between town and countryside, civilized society and the chaotic wilds of untamed nature. In many ways wolves epitomize the wild, that part of the world that humans cannot control, and in these stories their invasion of Tecpán symbolically foreshadowed the massive disruption of normative ("cultural") patterns of everyday life brought on by the earthquake. Were there really wolves on the streets that February day in 1976? We cannot say for sure. Several Tecpanecos we have talked to claim to have seen them; others are less sure, passing along stories that they have heard second- or third-hand. It is possible that wolves did wander into Tecpán that day; perhaps pre-seismic activity disturbed them and caused their unusual behavior (think of the many stories of animals acting strangely before a natural disaster). What is most important is not the veracity—from our perspective—of the story, but its function in contemporary Tecpán culture, what it means to people today. The story is compelling and worthy of being repeated because of its cathartic value in explaining the seemingly inexplicable question: Why us? Through such stories Tecpanecos maintain a collective historical memory that binds them together by reinforcing common perceptions.

Figure 4.2   Adding a second story onto one of Tecpán's nicer houses.

In national reconstruction efforts after the earthquake, the heavily damaged central highland towns were divvied up among international aid groups. The Salvation Army was assigned to Tecpán and came in with helicopters, big cargo choppers loaded down with sardines (which sticks out in people's minds) and canned fruits and vegetables, and then a little later clothing. The helicopters would land on the soccer field at the edge of town, and distribution of goods, at least in the early days, was haphazard at best. Women vividly recall scrambling into the helicopters to grab the last boxes of food or clothes, with the clothes sometimes turning out to be inappropriate for the person into whose hands they fell. Dresses were often deemed unacceptable by Maya women, even in these emergency situations, and the occasional pair of high heeled shoes or wig proved entirely useless. However, the vast majority of donations were put to use, even if years later. In 1980, Carol had the experience of working with women on sewing projects that included converting remaining earthquake relief pieces—an orange Hardy's restaurant shirt or a linen calendar towel from 1975—into serviceable children's clothing.

Rebuilding Tecpán was a slow process. In the days and weeks immediately following the quake and its aftershocks, people spent the nights sleeping in open spaces and the days sifting through the remains of their homes, searching for the few possessions that might have managed to avoid destruction. Memories are vivid of a favorite toy crushed or a set of plates spared by a fallen house. Bare hands and heavy machinery cleared housing sites so that construction could begin again. Without insurance, people were reduced to rebuilding their homes bit by bit and often had to start out with the cheapest, simplest materials until money was saved for more expensive constructions. Years after the quake it was still common to see houses made of odd pieces of sheet metal, cardboard, and rough slats of wood as well as portions of families' backyards covered with the patterned tiles of what had been the floors of larger and quite elegant pre-earthquake homes. (See Figure 4.2.)

In less than one decade Tecpán was to see two forms of extreme violence. In terms of the sheer number of dead, cumulative property loss, and the physical impact on each and every Tecpaneco, the brand of destruction that nature inflicted on the town in 1976 was without parallel. However, the cause of the destruction was understood as falling totally outside of human hands and subject to either religious explanation ("*Solo Díos sabe . . . *" "Only God knows . . . ") or scientific rationale (tectonic plates, fault lines, etc.). While the politics of aid and assistance kicked in soon enough, there were no human motives, political divisions, or international intrigue seen in the precipitating events, that is, the actual earthquake jolts. This meant not only that the destruction was literally visible all around town but the analyses of events were open, public, and subject to collective commentary. The destruction that was to hit Tecpán five or six years later was a significantly different sort, something without such a visual character and not as huge but which, one could argue, produced deeper fissures in the community.

La Violencia

Guatemala was a dangerous place in the late 1970s and early 1980s. Embroiled in *la violencia* (as it is now known, or *la situación* as it was termed at the time), Guatemala's escalating civil war pitted the state and army against several independent guerrilla groups. During that time, 100 to 200 people a month in Guatemala City were "disappeared," the euphemism used to describe kidnapping and murder by unknown persons (although most often assumed to be associated with organs of the state). Newspapers inconsistently reported the quantities of bodies found abandoned by the side of the road or, even less frequently, buried in clandestine graves. Villages in the countryside suspected of collaborating with guerrilla forces were literally erased from the landscape; some 440 burned to the ground in a scorched earth policy inspired by U.S. strategies for fighting the Viet Cong guerrillas during the Vietnam War (Schirmer 1998). In large parts of the country people lived in a state of constant fear. They never knew when strangers might show up at their door to take a family member away, when soldiers might attack a community (in the most brutal cases, stabbing pregnant women, slamming babies' heads against a wall, and burning people alive), or when a bus might be stopped by soldiers accompanied by a "guerrilla informant" wearing a ski mask, who would walk down the aisle and point out collaborators to be taken away for "questioning" (a common euphemism for torture). This random element to the violence exacerbated the terror felt by individuals. Kidnappers and assailants were often not clearly identifiable as guerrillas, soldiers, or members of one of the paramilitary groups with ties to the government, all of whom wore generic black ski masks and employed similar techniques. Thus, even though most of the violence might be securely attributed to the state, it was rarely known for sure exactly why someone was kidnapped and/or killed. Such uncertainty engendered a need for constant vigilance in everyday life, a carefulness with words even among family and close friends. A person never knew what innocent comment or action might be interpreted as support for the guerrillas or when a personal misunderstanding might result in an individual being accused as a subversive to the military.

During *la violencia,* a dominant way in which the army, in concert with the state propaganda machine, portrayed rural Indians was as potential subversives and thus deserving targets of military action. Genocidal slaughter and the wholesale destruction of Indian communities was subtly justified as necessary for a greater common good. First, apologists for the violence pointed to the example of pre-Hispanic Maya society, arguing that modern Indians are the descendants of the same Maya who ripped the hearts out of prisoners' still living bodies, who practiced self-mutilation, and who were fearless rulers. Second, it was noted that there was a kernel of socialism within many Maya traditions, a hint of Marx's primitive communism; that Indian communities held property in common was an affront to capitalism's pillar of private property. An irony here was that Peace Corps volunteers from the United States were supporting the development and ongoing operation of cooperatives, organizations labeled "socialist" and "subversive" during that time. Finally, it was suggested that Indians are ignorant, too bound to traditional lifeways, and easily duped by silver-tongued guerrilla leaders espousing communist rhetoric.

Ostensibly this was a battle of grand ideologies, of communists and socialists versus democrats and capitalists, but in practice it was disturbingly corporeal and personal. It was true state terrorism: government violence committed against a large population with the goal of instilling a deep-seated fear of reprisal. And it was disturbingly effective. A person never quite knew what might be considered a subversive act, and the violence became a means through which interpersonal conflicts could be resolved with impunity. Ironically these horrible acts—even the most clandestine—served in part as quasi-public messages to people not physically touched, the very ones who then felt the need to be guarded in talking about them in public. Even today, people speak of the violence rarely, and then most commonly in the privacy of their homes and only with individuals whom they trust.

Tecpán's Catholic priest in the late 1970s and early 1980s, Carlos Alberto Gálvez Galindo, was a *ladino* man of fairly progressive political and social views, not a radical by any means, but a man nonetheless who condemned discrimination against the Maya people and even made the effort of learning some Kaqchikel and using it in his work with parishioners. One Sunday in early May 1981 while saying mass, Padre Carlos spoke critically of the government, then, fearing the consequences of his words, left the town for several days. On Thursday, May 14, Tecpán's principal market day, the priest returned to say mass and baptize children, as was his weekly custom. Upon entering the rectory, he found his living quarters had been ransacked and, when he left there to make the short walk to the church, two young men in masks approached him from the market crowd. One stepped forward and shot Padre Carlos point blank in the head, killing him instantly in front of scores of people. The men escaped on motorcycle and were never caught; however, rumors circulated claiming that the priest's death was ordered by a low-level general in the army (this despite the fact that Padre Carlos had a brother who was a higher-ranking officer) or that the young men were associated with a government-backed paramilitary group that targeted the priest for his progressive views and with an eye on sending a message to townspeople couched in the rhetoric of religion to guard against guerrilla sympathies. Much later, people told of a young widow crying on the grave of her recently killed husband, lamenting that "this is what the government does to people who kill for it."

In November 1981, guerrillas responded to the murder of the priest by occupying Tecpán's town center for most of one day, holding all of the municipal officials in the town hall before dynamiting the building and shooting up the police station, jail, post office, and health center, which surround the main plaza. The mayor and other top officials were killed. One man recalls being on his way to catch a bus into the city around mid-day. As he approached the town square he heard much commotion, followed by a number of gunshots. Seeing people fleeing, he crawled underneath a nearby bus, and soon heard two massive explosions that shook the ground. After finally managing to make it back home, he returned the next day to find the town hall in ruins and many of the other plaza buildings damaged.

As is common in guerrilla warfare, rebels frequently targeted government buildings in rural communities for destruction, inflicting both symbolic and material damage on their enemy. For the rebels, lofty revolutionary ends justified their tactics, but for people in towns like Tecpán the results were devastating. Not only were crucial public services suspended, but such attacks inevitably led the army to suspect that the town was home to guerrilla sympathizers. Indeed, soon after this attack, the military set up a garrison on an open plot of land just off of the northwest corner of the town square. It was a makeshift affair, perhaps reflecting the army's view that this period of siege would not last long. As the violence dragged on, the military eventually moved into the former Casa de Cultura, alongside the soccer field on the outskirts of town.

The violence both allowed and masked corruption in Tecpán. For example, one of the town's "civilian military officials" (informants and local organizers for the army) used his military connections to extort money from families around town, promising to keep family members' names off of the black lists turned over to the local army garrison. One woman recalls the man coming into her small shop, taking things at will without paying for them, and demanding large sums of cash to protect her children from being kidnapped and killed. She always paid, but never mentioned it to her family, fearful that if they knew they would do something rash that would get them killed.

The violence and military occupation disrupted daily life in Tecpán in many ways. It was no longer even safe to cultivate fields located in outlying hamlets, as the harvest could be seen as food for guerrilla troops. Untold numbers of people were kidnapped, tortured, and killed. Twenty clandestine graves are known in the area around Tecpán, and it is likely that the actual number is much higher. Many families fled Tecpán and its dangers, some living temporarily in the mountains, most drawn to the anonymity of big city life in the capital. One Kaqchikel woman explains that leaving was much easier for *ladinos*: "They are not attached to Tecpán or even their own lands, they can just sell their houses and move . . . [and] they quickly forget Tecpán when they leave." In contrast, she continued, an Indian forced to flee inevitably left behind a piece of his heart and would always feel a pull to return home.

Tecpanecos, even today, are very reticent to discuss the violence and its effects in town. In part perhaps this is due to an understandable desire to forget what happened, to move on with their lives. But it also reflects the long-lasting effectiveness of the army's campaign of terror—the years of harsh conditioning to hold one's thoughts and to refrain from any criticism of the state are present in the loaded silences of conversation about the period. And lest one forget the lesson, the army is still around, patrolling the streets, silently observing public festivals, target practicing within hearing distance of the town center.

Yet reference to the violence does appear in conversations in the form of metaphorical discourse, the telling of stories that anthropologists generally classify as folklore. For example, a number of Tecpanecos report that during the violence of 1981 the town was invaded by monkeys, which roamed the streets at night making strange noises and banging on doors and walls. These are eerie stories, reflecting the same sort of premonitions found in the accounts of wolves howling before the 1976 earthquake. And they serve a similar psychological function: attempting to explain and come to terms with disconcertingly cabalistic events in culturally familiar terms. Such explanations are common responses to situations of great stress, offering a comfortable ideological anchor in a dramatically unstable world. Monkey stories are particularly interesting given the important role of monkeys in both ancient and modern Maya cosmologies. The *Popol Vuh* tells of earlier failed attempts by the gods to make human beings; when the people made of sticks in the third creation failed to offer praise to their creators, they were turned into monkeys and left to live in the forests.

Monkey stories that echo *Popol Vuh* themes are regularly told in Tecpán. For example, Tecpanecos tell of a particular older man living in town who is able to change himself into a monkey, which he does late at night and looks for lost souls to seduce with his evil magic; never married and living by himself, he flaunts local social norms and, when relatives forced him to have his hair cut some years back, the barber is said to have mysteriously died several days later. During Carnival celebrations in the Tzotzil Maya town of Chamula (in Chiapas, Mexico), men dressed as monkeys play an important disruptive function, heckling the other dancers dressed as Spaniards, Moors, and Maya princes, and goading onlookers (see Bricker 1973; Gossen 1999). Here, as in the stories from Tecpán, monkeys play a symbolically liminal role; that is, they represent the opposite of accepted cultural norms and are thus a threat to established tradition. The term *liminality* was coined by Arnold van Gennep in an early study of rites of passage to describe the period between social stages; the concept was further developed by Victor Turner (1969), who described liminality as a state of "betwixt and between" in which normal social rules do not apply. Liminality is a necessary state of certain social conditions, but it is a potentially dangerous state for societies as conventional norms are contested. And it is precisely this danger that adds poignancy to the stories of monkeys invading Tecpán, stories that make culturally comprehensible (if no less terrorizing) the new dangers brought on by the war. The cries of monkeys roaming the streets at night symbolically echo the cries of torture victims taken to the army base for questioning, announcing the chaotic terror of daily life.

Kay Warren (1993), an anthropologist who works in San Andrés Semetebaj, a Kaqchikel town that borders Tecpán on the southwest, records a story that serves a similar function. "Peel Off Flesh, Come Back On" tells of a man whose wife begins to act mysteriously, always sick and exhausted. One night the man wakes up to find not his wife but a grinding stone lying next to him in bed, and, with the aid of a diviner, he plots to find out what she is doing in the middle of the night. He stays up one night, pretending to be fast asleep, and watches in disgust as his wife peels off her flesh and turns into a grotesque animal, who leaves to roam the streets. He eventually tricks his wife—herself a trickster—by pouring salt on the pile of flesh she leaves behind when she makes her magical transformation. When she returns home, she is unable to put back on the dead flesh and leaves forever. This story builds on long-standing Mesoamerican beliefs about multiple souls, the ability of individuals to transform themselves, and the sorts of power to which women have recourse. When told in the 1980s and early 1990s, such stories were also apparent allusions to the indeterminacy of life during the violence. As Warren remarks, "for the Kaqchikel Mayans, these accounts describe a world parallel to their current situation—one of betrayal and existential dilemmas" (1993: 46).

Tecpán, like most Maya towns, is home to a number of saints' images, generally statues of the saints that are kept in the church and in various private houses. The most important of these (and there is a complex system of ranking the relative importance of saints) are the images of Saint Francis of Assisi, the town's patron saint, although others are also kept by religious brotherhoods known as *cofradías* (see Chapter 6). Within this hierarchy, one image occupies a unique position. Called

Weapons of the Weak

The political scientist James Scott coined the phrase "weapons of the weak" to describe how putatively disempowered groups subtly exert political and economic power. Studying rice farmers in a Malaysian village in the late 1970s, Scott found them engaged in a fight for their livelihood against mechanized rice harvesting, which was being introduced in the area with the backing of the government and international organizations. Mechanization favored very large farms and put laborers out of work, but given the militarization of the Malaysian state (not unlike that in Guatemala), overt resistance would be deadly. Thus, Scott shows, Malaysian peasants employed weapons of the weak in their battle: foot dragging at work (costing employers money), false compliance and feigned ignorance ("those stupid peasants, I have to tell them to do something five times before it actually gets done"), pilfering, and spreading gossip and slander. Scott's model is so appealing because it is so widely applicable. These same sorts of techniques are used in labor disputes in which employees cannot afford to give up their jobs; in university settings where students attempt to exert power vis-à-vis professors and the administration; and among poor Tecpanecos to critique social inequalities in an indirect (and thus deniable) manner.

The concept of weapons of the weak ties into a growing concern in anthropology with what is called the *subaltern*. The concept of subaltern was adopted by the Italian Marxist Antonio Gramsci (the bulk of whose work is notebooks he wrote in prison in the 1920s) to refer to subjugated groups in a society (for Gramsci, mainly peasants and workers). In Gramsci's influential scheme, the subaltern stands in contrast to the *hegemonic*, and he revealed how a society's dominant class exerts hegemonic power over subaltern populations through the often subtle ideological biases of popular culture, mass media, education, and religion. While discussions of the term abound, a useful definition of *hegemony* is "an order in which a certain way of life and thought is dominant, in which one concept of reality is diffused throughout society in all its institutional and private manifestations, informing with its spirit all taste, morality, customs, religious and political principles, and all social relations, particularly in their intellectual and moral connotation" (G. Williams in Eley 1994: 320–321). As an academic subdiscipline, subaltern studies grew out of revisionist ethnographic and historical research on rural India, as seen in the works of Ranajit Guha and Partha Chatterjee, although its perspectives are increasingly being used in work on Latin America and others parts of the world. (For a discussion on Latin America, see Mallon 1994.)

Maxutio (and known as Maximon in other towns), he is a hybrid Judas figure celebrated (or rather reviled) on Good Friday. In the 1970s, the Maxutio image (which, unlike the others, is made anew each year) would be paraded through town, winding up on the steps in front of the Catholic Church, where his handlers would read lists of gossip and jesting accusations against prominent town figures. The mayor, who was widely believed to have been illegally selling lumber from communal forests, was brought to task by Maxutio, as were local businessmen who gouged their customers, overbearing evangelical preachers, fraternizing husbands, and corrupt school officials. After the year's list of accusations had been read to the jeering crowd, the figure of Maxutio (clothing stuffed with pine straw, with a mask and hat attached) was ceremonially hung and then burned.

The Maxutio celebration was just the sort of resistance James Scott had in mind when he coined the term "weapons of the weak" (see box). Effective because of the jesting nature of the presentations—serious accusation, but not fighting words, and always couched in the veil of satire—the Maxutio tradition provided an outlet for collective social sanctions against individuals to be expressed, filling a void of legal recourse. Celebrating a Judas-figure on Good Friday is an intriguing twist in the normal Catholic ritual calendar, invoking the treachery of the corrupt disciple as well as the passion of Jesus, a man said to have died for telling the truth. Maxutio celebrations ended in 1981 with another brutal death at the hands of authorities, the kidnapping and murder of the man who ran the loose organization that sponsored Maxutio festivities. An outspoken critic of the state and active in several local cultural and political organizations, he was taken from his home one night as his wife watched in terror; his body was later found mutilated by the side of a road. Maxutio was not paraded again for more than ten years, but in 1994 the tradition was revived, *sans* the public political commentary, which was probably a good thing as soldiers lingered around the edge of the crowd as it paraded through town.

Folklore and gossip also serve Tecpanecos as effective weapons of the weak. For example, the owner of the Veloz Poaquileña bus line is Don Eustacio, a wealthy Indian businessman rumored to have made a Faustian pact with a demon. With an air of conspiratorial insider knowledge, some Tecpanecos tell of a strong box filled with gold and jewels that is only visible to Don Eustacio. Once, it was reported, thieves broke into his home to steal the box, but when they broke the lock and pried open the top they discovered only snakes. Accounts such as this—and others that vary on the theme, take different tacks, or contradict it—form a salient genre of Tecpaneco storytelling. Indeed, cognate tales are recorded from throughout the Maya region, invoking the darker side of the reciprocity that underwrites relations between humans and spirit beings (see Chapter 3). In the Tecpán context, they reflect a fundamental ambivalence toward wealth. On the one hand, Tecpanecos generally admire hard work and respect economic advancement as its just (if elusive) reward. At the same time, there is a deep suspicion of excessive wealth and monopolistic business practices ripe for abuse. With

Don Eustacio's virtual monopoly on local bus service and Tecpanecos' relative helplessness to contest his power, stories that impugn his moral character (making a deal with the demon to get rich at the expense of his upstanding compatriots) serve as both a psychological vent and a social force uniting those who tell, listen to, then pass along the account.

CULTURAL REVITALIZATION

Indigenous culture itself can be used as an effective "weapon of the weak" in much more subtle ways than the Maxutio celebrations. In the 1970s, before the silencing effect of the violence, Tecpán was an important center of Indian organizing. Throughout the Guatemalan highlands this was a time of ethnic awakening for Indians, as young Maya men and women took a renewed and self-conscious interest in their cultural heritage, and numerous local and regional organizations sprang up to promote Maya issues, including linguistic and cultural study groups, theater troupes, queens contests, and political associations. In 1974 Fernando Tezagüic Tohón, a Kaqchikel man from Tecpán, was elected to Congress along with Pedro Verona Cúmez, a Kaqchikel candidate from the neighboring town of Comalapa. Both men created a stir in the chambers by wearing traditional Maya dress (for males, shin length white pants held up by a pink, green, blue, and white belt; a woven wool apron (*rodillero*) stretching from waist to above the knee; a white shirt; a dark jacket; and sandals) and opening their speeches with a few words in Kaqchikel. In Quetzaltenango, Guatemala's second largest city and historically home to a large class of prosperous Indian merchants, a Maya political party was formed to support a candidate for mayor in the 1976 elections. A group based in Comalapa founded a magazine, *Ixim,* to promote pan-Maya pride.

In Tecpán two principal organizations were begun by young Maya in the mid–1970s, the Asociación de Profesionales Indígenas de Tecpán and the Círculo Juvenil Ixmucané. The former had an older, more established membership (indigenous professionals, mostly men but with a few women, establishing or advancing in their careers), while the latter was a group of younger men and women, some still in school or with less formal education (some were also the younger siblings of Profesionales Indígenas). One young man, smart and impassioned about ethnic issues but who never finished his high school education because he had to work in the fields with his father, recalls desperately trying to fit in with the Profesionales Indígenas but never being really accepted; when the Círculo Ixmucané formed he quickly joined and was an active member until forced to flee from the violence in 1981. Despite their slightly different constituencies, both groups were dedicated to like goals: promoting ethnic pride and creating a sanctioned public space for Maya culture in Tecpán and Guatemalan society more broadly. The means to these ends were likewise similarly conceived, spoken of in terms of "self-improvement," "auto-formation," and "training "—developing themselves (individually and collectively) to better engage national structures. Participants read and discussed books, Maya texts as well as academic treatises on the Guatemalan situation; members of the Circulo Ixmucané produced a short play that was presented in the surrounding villages; and one offshoot group started an experimental farm just outside of town.

Leadership and organizational skills developed through these groups played an important role in Tecpán's mobilization after the earthquake. Local Maya activists played central roles in reconstruction efforts and set up organizations to help administer the aid monies flowing in for rebuilding the town. But by the early 1980s, the violence had reached the point that any public promotion of Maya culture or grassroots organization was seen as suspect, and both groups disbanded. Many of the former members were forced to flee Tecpán altogether, as they were prime candidates for the death lists being compiled. A number went to the anonymity of the capital, where they met with like-minded exiles from other parts of the country and organized several underground culture groups.

As the violence began to subside in 1984, a number of Maya groups were formed in the capital and suddenly were able to come out in the open. They became part of the nascent pan-Maya movement in Guatemala. Such groups were careful to keep their focus on "nonpolitical" issues, such as cultural preservation (in a folkloric sense) and linguistic revival. Nonetheless, it is surprising that the pan-Maya movement, based as it is on a philosophy of Indian pride and self-determination, would emerge so quickly from the ashes of Guatemala's devastation. However, one Maya day-keeper (a traditional religious specialist) from Tecpán explains that Maya resurgence is not surprising in the least. In fact it is the logical outcome of *la violencia*, the return for the great sacrifice Maya people made:

> How many thousands of people died? Thousands, not hundreds, died. They were buried just anywhere as if they were animals. The blood of these people went to the earth and was consummated before God, right? This blood is their spirit, right? Thus our people have now won—and we remember how it was before. We already paid and gave alms . . . it is much better now.

Maya cultural revitalization efforts began by working for the conservation and resurrection of elements of Maya culture. By the late 1990s Maya leaders were bolder in calling for political reforms to promote ethnic equality within Guatemalan society (calls that would have been met with death threats not so many years earlier). Their accomplishments are impressive: Legislative reforms have been pushed through that favor Mayan languages, Maya groups were given a formal role in peace negotiations between the government and rebels, and a burgeoning Maya intelligentsia has produced much valuable research. Organizations within the movement produce newspapers, magazines, and radio programs in Mayan languages with a focus on Maya culture; hieroglyphic writing has been resurrected and is frequently used to date Maya publications and number pages; a growing number of individuals are taking Maya names for themselves, most borrowed from precontact historical figures or their date of birth in the Maya calendar; and some young Maya men are growing their hair long and wearing it in a ponytail in the style of Classic Maya portraits.

The Maya movement is led by a well-educated and relatively affluent group of professional scholars, activists, and politicians. One of the most surprising features of this group is the preponderance of Kaqchikeles from Tecpán. The story of Demetrio Cojtí Cuxil, considered by most the reigning intellectual of contemporary Maya activism, is exemplary. Born in 1948 and raised in an *aldea* of Tecpán, Cojtí was able to complete his secondary studies (no small feat for a rural Maya boy at the time). Then, with the help of a Belgian priest assigned to Tecpán at that time, he obtained a scholarship to attend the University of Louvain in Belgium, where he earned his doctorate. In the mid 1970s he was an important yet marginal figure in Tecpán's cultural organizations—owing in part to his studies abroad as well as activities in Guatemala City when he was home—and participants remember him coming to town to give lectures, a captivating orator even in his late twenties. After receiving his Ph.D. in communications in 1980, Cojtí returned to Guatemala to pursue a number of teaching and public service positions. Living in the capital throughout the 1980s and 1990s, Cojtí worked primarily as a consultant to UNICEF, advising on programs of education and health for Maya children. Starting with a short essay in the *Revista Cultural de Guatemala* (1984), titled "Problemas de la identidad nacional guatemalteca," Cojtí has written a series of influential articles and books that critique the neo-colonial structures of Guatemalan national society. In them he presents a wealth of cultural and linguistic as well as political and economic data to make increasingly bold demands for reform within the Guatemalan state (see Cojtí Cuxil 1990, 1991, 1994, 1997). His analyses of Guatemalan "neo-colonialism" and vision for the future of Maya peoples (positions for which he would likely have been killed in the early 1980s) have broadly set the agenda for pan-Maya activism. Cojtí—who now also publishes under the Maya name Waqi' Q'anil—was appointed vice minister for education in 2000, a move that speaks both to his stature as a public intellectual and to the growing power of an ethnically aware Maya electorate. While he continues to reside in the capital, his parents both still live in Tecpán, and he regularly returns to visit the community.

Similarly, Raxche' (Demetrio Rodríguez Guaján), now in his early forties, grew up in Tecpán, was active in local cultural groups in the 1970s, and determined to complete his education. After working in the reconstruction effort in 1976 and 1977, he obtained a scholarship to study in Canada for four months with a group of other Guatemalan youths. He recalls the Canadian English teacher starting class one day by saying, "Spanish is a stupid language: stupid, stupid, stupid. A table does not have a gender." Among his *ladino* classmates, he was the only one to eagerly agree (like English, Kaqchikel does not employ grammatical gender).

Raxche' was much impressed by the standard of living in Canada ("even the poor farmers lived nicely, with their own cars and televisions") and complained aloud to his peers that it was wasting money to send them to Canada when there is so much poverty in Guatemala. Today, Raxche' traces a dramatic shift in his ethnic consciousness to his experiences in Canada, where he saw first-hand other, more just, social possibilities. This recalls Arjun Appadurai's (1996) discussion of the imagination in the globalized world. Exposure to different ways of looking at the world (made more commonplace by communication and transportation advances) expand the individual and collective imagination. We have traditionally conflated imagination and fantasy, seeing them as means to escape reality, but Appadurai notes that "the imagination is today a staging ground for action, and not only for escape"(1996: 7). Since his return to Guatemala, Raxche' has helped found a Maya editorial house and publishing company, has published several articles and books on topics ranging from Maya numeration systems to culturally sensitive economic development (see Raxche' 1996), and currently directs Guatemala's bilingual education program.

José Serech, another Tecpaneco of the generation that came of age in the 1960s and 1970s, also studied abroad, in the Philippines and the United States; he now heads the Center for Maya Research and Documentation. Similar stories mark the life histories of many other Tecpán men (and it is mostly men, although by the late 1990s an increasing number of women were getting involved) active in the pan-Maya movement.

It is therefore somewhat surprising that one finds very little grassroots cultural activism in Tecpán today, at least not in the sense of public initiatives aimed at promoting identity issues. There have been a few hieroglyphic workshops given in town, and there seems to be some interest in learning the basics of this ancient writing system. A few grassroots groups have formed to promote cultural activities and political activism, with very modest results. Maya religious specialists (day-keepers, diviners, healers) are increasing in number and prominence in the aftermath of the violence, when their trade was suspect. And, in contrast to decades past, Kaqchikel is taught in some schools so that children have an opportunity to study a language that they might not have learned from birth. For the most part, however, there is little sign of the very conscious, public expression of Maya pride that leaders in the capital are advocating. Most of Tecpanecos concerned with these sorts of Maya cultural issues and initiatives live in Guatemala City, where there are more opportunities for professional advancement and lobbying government.

To explain this seeming lack some people claim, derisively, that Tecpanecos are too concerned with making money to devote themselves to cultural pursuits. There is undoubtedly something to be said for this, for Tecpán's Maya as well as *ladino* citizens. However, pride in being Maya finds expression in multiple forms, and among the noteworthy consequences of cultural revitalization in Guatemala are more conscious and overt articulations of what it means to be Indian in a variety of contexts (the majority extremely mundane) as well as critical assessments of what others are doing. Thus, some Maya living in Tecpán point to those in Guatemala City and claim that the latter are interested in making money off their ethnicity and being celebrity Indians: "They're more Maya than the Maya," an indigenous Tecpaneco said, comparing the contemporary Maya activists in the capital with the Maya of the Classic Era. Protestant Indians often think that Maya religious specialists are *brujos* (witches) and their practices *brujería* (witchcraft) aimed at doing harm, while some Catholic Indians are extremely uncomfortable with religious practices that the church doesn't condone. And lessons in hieroglyphics or even the Kaqchikel language can be criticized as backwards-looking and not what a person needs to get along in today's world.

Criticisms like these do not, however, mean that the person articulating the concerns rejects being Maya. In Tecpán, hundreds and hundreds of Maya men who don't wear *traje*, children who don't speak Kaqchikel fluently, and families that would never go to a Maya diviner still consider themselves unquestionably Maya and suffer the prejudices of a larger world that sees them as Indian and hence inferior. Being Maya is a complex social phenomenon having to do with blood and heritage, social practices and cultural meanings, and maybe even some physical attributes. These are issues that we examine more closely in subsequent chapters having to do with subjects such as language, dress, socialization, religion, and the sense of self and group.

Further Reading

Carlsen, Robert S. 1997. *The war for the heart and soul of a highland Maya town*. Austin: University of Texas Press.

Cojtí Cuxil, Demetrio. 1996. The politics of Maya revindication. In *Maya cultural activism in Guatemala*, edited by Edward F. Fischer and R. McKenna Brown, pp. 719–50. Austin: University of Texas Press.

Paul, Benjamin D., and William J. Demarest. 1988. The operation of a death squad in San Pedro La Laguna. In *Harvest of violence: The Maya Indians and the Guatemalan crisis*, edited by Robert M. Carmack, pp. 119–154. Norman: University of Oklahoma Press.

Raxche'(Demetrio Rodríguez Guaján). 1996. Maya culture and the politics of development. In *Maya cultural activism in Guatemala*, edited by Edward F. Fischer and R. McKenna Brown, pp. 74–88. Austin: University of Texas Press.

Warren, Kay B. 1998. *Indigenous movements and their critics: Pan-Maya activism in Guatemala*. Princeton, NJ: Princeton University Press.

A Maya ceremony conducted at an unexcavated mound on the grounds of the Iximche' archaeological park outside Tecpán.

5

Kaqchikel Hearts, Souls, and Selves: Competing Religions and Worldviews

A common topic of conversation in Tecpán involves spiritual paths to a religious community and a set of religious beliefs that feel comfortable to an individual (and that help with family issues, alcoholism, poor health, and other such problems). The religious affiliations of Tecpanecos are far from homogeneous: Almost 60 percent consider themselves Catholic and over 35 percent identify as Evangelical Protestant, with practitioners of traditionalist Maya religion overlapping significantly with a segment of the Catholics and to a lesser extent with Protestants. Mormons and Mennonites also make up part of the religious "mix." Although the religious possibilities found in Tecpán may seem abundant for a town of 10,000, these are not the only frames for grappling with questions such as "What does it mean to be human?" "Who am I?" and "How can I lead a more satisfying life?" For example, what originally might have been analyzed and labeled within a "secular" frame could, over time, come to be reconceptualized and relabeled in more "religious" terms (although locally people might never make a distinction like this). We have both had conversations in Tecpán where people referred to medical doctors, psychology books, and self-help treatises as alternative means. What is more, many of the terms and themes that emerge forcefully as being "religious" in nature also have more secular sides. For example, people mundanely refer to the *carácter* of someone, the power of a man with "strong blood," or the effect of a traumatic event on a little boy's *nervios* ("nerves"). These might be treated by a ritual specialist, or perhaps by the grandmother of the family who knows the right herbal cure, a medical doctor would prescribe a drug or the mother of the family may buy a bottle of over-the-counter medicine for calming nerves.

A DOMINANT FRAME FOR DEFINING
THE ESSENTIAL (MAYA) PERSON

Kaqchikel conceptions of the self influence how people look at the world in subtle and profound ways. But these conceptions are open to active interpretation, and individuals deploy them in varying contexts and toward varying ends. In traditionalist Kaqchikel belief everyone has both a heart (*k'u'x*) and a soul (*anima*), and the two are central to Kaqchikel notions of the self. Everything is said to possess *k'u'x*, but only humans have the vitalistic force of *anima*, and that is what makes them human. The distinction between *k'u'x* and *anima* helps us understand the fine distinction made in many Maya beliefs between fate (or destiny) and individual volition. *K'u'x* is often translated into English (or Spanish) as "heart" (*corazón*), "soul"(*alma*), "center" (*centro*), or "essence" (*esencia*), and this range of meaning gives a sense of the semantic variation the term encompasses.

Although many Kaqchikel Tecpanecos hold these abstract cultural ideals (or senses similar to them), a certain segment of the population who are identified as "traditionalists" operationalize them through specific social practice and ritual. For example, there is the notion that everyone is born with a *k'u'x*. The *k'u'x* is especially fragile in the early days of life, and some new parents conduct a ceremony nine days after the birth to "seat" the child's *k'u'x* by burying ("planting") the umbilical cord. From such a traditionalist perspective, the *k'u'x* possesses certain characteristics (elements of what we might call personality) based on the divinatory connotations of the day on which one was born, a sign of the conjuncture of cosmic forces that affects individuals. But one's *k'u'x* changes during one's lifetime, affected by myriad quotidian experiences as well as dramatic life history events (the death of a relative, an earthquake, the violence). All of these factors are said to shape one's *k'u'x* and thus shape one's predisposition in the world.

To have a big *k'u'x* (*nim ruk'u'x*) is to be honest, trustworthy, and reliable, a good-hearted and kind person; to have a small *k'u'x* implies the opposite. A person possessing a hard *k'u'x* is insensitive to the concerns of others and thoroughly self-interested; at the same time, to have too soft or malleable a heart is a sign of moral and physical weakness. These are not hard and fast categories so much as salient, if extreme, ideals, and such designations are usually applied situationally and to a specific action. To have one's *k'u'x* go to another person is to fall in love, a potentially blissful state, but one that can also threaten the equilibrium of the heart. A normal Kaqchikel is said to have a content (i.e., grounded and centered) *k'u'x* (*nik'ikot ruk'u'x*), denoting a deep-seated social and psychological stability.

The concept of *k'u'x* is intimately related to that of *anima*. *Anima* is most likely a loan word adopted from the Spanish *anima* ("spirit"), and it seems to have replaced the Kaqchikel term *natub* found in early colonial dictionaries (Hill and Fischer 1999). *Anima* is conceived as a life force unique to humans, as that which animates human action (mental as well as physical). "It is what makes us human," an older woman explains, "it gives us the will and power to live." The *anima* is affected by the underlying predispositions of the *k'u'x*; conversely, the *k'u'x* is affected by one's *anima*. Through *anima* the predispositions of the *k'u'x* are enacted and made real. A person with a strong *anima* is active, a go-getter, but *anima* doesn't only motivate positive behavior. Violent individuals, alcoholics, and witches, for example, are often said to have a strong *anima*, and thus are able to resist the norms imposed by the community to pursue their own self-interests. Pregnant women also have strong *anima*, just as they can be described as having "strong blood" or being "hot," the latter referring to an extreme of the hold-cold continuum that overlaps with the humoral notions of hot and cold that came with the Spanish and are found today throughout Latin America. One woman, Doña Eulalia, described the exceptional power of the *anima* of pregnant women with a story about her mother. Carrying her younger brother, Doña Eulalia's mother was frightened one day as she stepped on a snake lying by the household well; she hurried indoors, urinated in a cup, and threw the urine on the snake, killing it instantly and restoring her *anima*. Doña Eulalia explained that so powerful is the heat of pregnancy, and so pervasive is it throughout the body, that the snake did not have a chance.

The *anima* can also leave the body or be stolen, often a very dangerous condition that can easily lead to death. Some say that dreams are a signal that the *anima* leaves a person, and it returns to the body only when it tires. Sometimes these nocturnal travels involve encounters with evil, and the *anima* engages in fights, which explains why people wake up sweaty and frightened sometimes. The very young, the elderly, and sick people are especially vulnerable to illnesses of the soul. A sudden scare (*susto* in Spanish)—being scared by a dog or an angry person, for example—can result in the *anima* fleeing in fright (*xb'e ranima*). There are also more extreme states of *susto*, such as those described by survivors in the aftermath of the violence (see Green 1999). When one's *anima* leaves, so does the desire to live. Within this frame of thought, death may be avoided through intervention, through rituals performed by an *aj q'ij* that involve a ritual bath in a river or stream, the water of which can bring back the soul of the afflicted (the *oyoj ruk'u'x* ceremony).

Anima is associated with both normality and abnormality, with an individual's behavior often interpreted in terms of the condition of his or her *anima*. A normal person is described as *nik'ikot ranima* (having a content or beautiful *anima*); an errant individual is *itzel ranima* (having an ugly *anima*) or *yalan kow ranima* (with a very hard *anima*, used to describe especially self-centered individuals). Unlike the *k'u'x*, the *anima* survives death and lives on as a disembodied soul, living in the heavens and/or on Earth. On All Saint's Day a few families still carry on the tradition of tying short messages to dead ancestors onto the tails of kites and flying the kites in the cemetery.

One's *k'u'x* is laid down in important ways at birth and further molded during early childhood and played out through the *anima*. Take the case of Kan, a rambunctious seven-year-old boy. His parents suspect that his unruly behavior is symptomatic of an unbalanced *k'u'x* and a misdirected *anima*, for Kan has had a hard life. The last of seven children, he came into the world in the midst of hard times for his family. His father was battling alcoholism, often leaving his mother, María, to scrape together enough money to buy a few tortillas to feed the children. María recalls Kan's infancy as a time of great desperation, she constantly at wit's end trying to hold her family together and unable to produce enough milk to feed little Kan. So distraught was she at one point that Kan became severely dehydrated and malnourished and had to be taken to the regional hospital.

Today, Kan's household is a picture of almost ideal familial harmony. His father has long since stopped drinking, and he is once again the fine man—kind, sincere, hardworking—that María married. Although always living week to week, family finances are back on keel, and the children are all doing well in school. All except for Kan, who frequently gets into fights, disrupts class, and throws loud fits when he does not get his way. It is feared that his early childhood experiences left his *k'u'x* (which, in the sense of the word used here, is what metaphysically grounds and centers the Kaqchikel self) dangerously unbalanced. To treat the problem, Kan's family employed the services of an *aj q'ij* ("day-keeper" or Maya religious specialist) to call back any missing parts of the boy's soul and to ground his *k'u'x* and recenter his *anima*. They all went to a small stream that runs along the edge of town, and there Kan was washed in the water, which returned missing parts of his soul and made it whole again. A short ceremony followed in which the *aj q'ij* offered praise to a long list of ancestors, gods, and saints (both Maya and Catholic), beseeching them to respond by helping Kan. Incense made from tree resin was burned, enveloping Kan's body in smoke, and he was ritually washed with aromatic leaves. In the months after the ceremony took place, Kan's family reported a noticeable improvement in Kan's demeanor, although not the sort of dramatic change they had hoped for.

Kan may have been born with a predisposition to soul loss, but this predisposition was realized through real world interactions, leading to his condition at the tender age of seven. Early dispositions are seen as especially resilient, and abnormal behavior may be classified as a revelation of one's true soul. And yet events throughout one's life, the sequence of unique events from which emerges the individual, also constantly affect the *k'u'x* just as they are affected by it; a system of feedback in which psychological and social predispositions interact with real world experiences (material constraints as well as the ideational predispositions of others) to produce situationally unique responses.

COMPLICATING TERMS AND MEANINGS

Key words such as *k'u'x* and *anima* that refer to the core being of a Kaqchikel person are complex and play an important role in the cultural meanings that are played out daily in highland social life. In all cases the terms have multiple layers of meaning that make giving them brief dictionary definitions enormously difficult. (See Laughlin 1975: 4–12, on the challenges of making a dictionary for another Mayan language.) Their full complexity is only revealed when considering real life instances where they are used, and in response to questions such as, Who is using the terms, With reference to whom, Who has done what, While talking with whom, Under what circumstances, and With what sort of history? In addition, it is necessary to know what language or languages a person speaks, his or her religious affiliation and attitudes toward others, and the other social frames that the person uses to think through particular cases (e.g., biomedical or psychological terms). As we have seen, although the majority of indigenous Tecpanecos speak Kaqchikel, a significant number speak mostly or only Spanish. The words used to characterize the essence of a person therefore can be in Kaqchikel or Spanish, with all the issues of translation and connotation attached to words that at some level might seem "the same" but at another level are significantly different.

John Watanabe has written on the Maya town of Santiago Chimaltenango and how its Mam-speaking inhabitants understand their distinctiveness. In discussing local senses of self, Watanabe describes *naab'l*, "a person's 'way of being'" or "soul" (1992: 254), as a constantly emergent construction, with the meanings given to a particular person's *naab'l* changing through real life social interactions. Even in a linguistically and religiously more homogeneous town than Tecpán, determining the different senses of a term like *naab'l* and what it means for people is a complicated task. However, this is not to say that the number of key concepts is simply multiplied by languages and religions present. Rather, there is a core of terms used by the majority of people whose overlapping and interrelated concepts are discussed and may be contested in terms of subtle but intensely meaningful differences among them. These differences reflect people's notions of health and well-being, sociability, destiny, respect, and/or constitution as well as the analysis and classification of the state of a person or persons in the first place.

Although the material just outlined represents a general sense of local understandings of *k'u'x* and *anima* for many Tecpanecos, "traditional Kaqchikel beliefs" are by no means monolithic, and the ways in which individuals conceive of their spirituality and religion vary significantly. This presents real difficulty for those of us who try to write ethnography: How can we represent the great on-the-ground diversity we have witnessed in a coherent narrative? Mokchewan, for example, is a young adult (born in the mid–1970s), a Kaqchikel speaker from birth, a member of the Catholic Church, and someone whose interest in Maya religion is growing.

He worked with Carol on Kaqchikel Mayan and, as part of her lessons, he recorded short pieces on various topics, which Carol then transcribed and translated. One of these was "*Ri anima*," words that he translated as *el alma* ("the soul") or *el espiritu* ("the spirit"). According to him, *ri anima* was "what we can't see" and the means by which people consult with the "our grandmothers and grandfathers." A person's *k'u'x* ("heart"), on the other hand, he described as "a part of the body that distributes blood throughout the body," a sense that seemed to come more from a biological than a spiritual frame. When Carol asked him about *k'u'x* and *anima* phrases, his comments suggested that, in these cases, the words weren't so much words or things in and of themselves or theological terms from a religious setting but more like elements of a larger phrase, the cultural senses and meanings about which he had abundant native-speaker insights. Thus, for example, when asked about the phrase *yalan kow ranima* (literally, "very hard-souled"), Mokchewan gave the example of a person on whose property is located a spring with clean well water; a "hard-souled" person would deny thirsty passersby a drink. For *nim ruk'u'x* he first said that it was a term used in weaving meaning that there was ample room between sheds to insert the shuttle and create another row of fabric. Only then did he mention that it also referred to a very kind or generous person.

In another case Carol talked with Don Mario, a man in the "elders" set (over seventy years old), a Tecpaneco and Kaqchikel speaker from birth, and also a Catholic who converted to Protestantism decades ago. Although Protestant Kaqchikeles have a range of reactions to the subject of traditional Maya practices, there are many who consciously define their beliefs in opposition to what they see as *brujería* (witchcraft) coded in certain practices and terms. Carol had just read an article by Ted that included information on caves such as Pulchich in the Tecpán area that are traditional Maya religious sites. The article also discussed various *k'u'x* phrases, and so Carol decided to ask Don Mario what he might know about these places and linguistic uses. Regarding the caves, Don Mario mentioned working in the area of Pulchich as a young man. He gave a description of the geography of the area, mentioned that the cave was dark when he looked in, and simply and without any indication of an attitude noted that that is where "*sacerines* [another word used to refer to Maya religious practitioners] go with their chickens." Following this exchange, in which Carol was fairly explicit in stating her interest in any religious dimensions, she turned to a discussion of *k'u'x* phrases and Don Mario's understandings of these. Here there was not the slightest hint that the subject might have any religious orientation. Rather, it seemed to be a sorting out of terms used from Tecpán versus neighboring communities or an inquiry into *costumbre*. Thus the term *ruk'u'x rumerya* (literally, "the heart of the money") elicited mention of the Kaqchikel word for "money" found in Patzún; that phrase, however, didn't mean anything for him. (Mokchewan said that it referred to a special coin that one would want to keep.) Don Mario did, however, mention the phrase *ruk'u'x jul* (where *jul* means "cave, pit, hole"), which was used to refer to a stone placed in the corn storage bin "so that the harvest is not consumed rapidly." This, he said, was something that people did when he was a little boy.

Maya concepts of the soul are born of lived experience. They are emergent, constantly built out of daily experience and practical activities. Their fluctuating, contingent nature is, however, constrained in important ways by collective memories and the cultural mandates and prohibitions passed down from the ancestors. The variations, recognitions, and nonrecognitions of meanings of these terms are loaded with commentary on what is going on in terms of Maya language and identity in Guatemala today.

Our discussion of these terms points out variations and multiple understandings of key words, some of which link to cosmological or spiritual issues while others touch upon very different spheres of Tecpanecos' lives. Thus it is with all cultural knowledge: Beliefs and understandings vary widely between individuals even in the same community, and yet there are important threads of commonality as well, at least enough to allow for effective communication. What *k'u'x* or *anima* or any other such word means changes (sometimes subtly, sometimes dramatically) from person to person, context to context; no one can know a word's full meaning and fewer still have the linguistic resources to subtly articulate these understandings. Often "linguistic meanings" emerge in conjunction with the actions associated with the words. In our own ongoing struggle to get at the meanings of key terms and cultural patterns, we think it best to turn to more "practice-oriented" examples and examine what meanings emerge "in action" to illuminate traditionalist Maya religion and associated issues of worldview.

MAYA RELIGIOUS AND HEALING SPECIALISTS

There are several types of Maya religious specialists, including some whose gifts move them into realms that we would consider medical. These include the *aj q'ij*, who is associated with divination and benevolent practices, the *aj itz'* ("witch"), who practices malevolent black magic, and the bone-setter and midwife, who combine both medical and religious services. All of these professions are considered to be callings, in the sense that one is destined to fulfill these tasks and fighting that destiny is almost impossible. Often, religious specialists speak of having suffered greatly before entering into training: an illness, nightmares, or other disturbing signs. They are usually called in a dream in which they are shown how to relieve their current sufferings.

It is difficult to write about "Maya religion" because, like other spiritual traditions, it is so nebulous and sometimes contradictory. Unlike the Judeo-Christian tradition, traditional Maya religion is not codified in texts. It is an oral tradition, passed down from generation to generation, individual to individual. Thus, ironically, while many anthropologists see in Maya religious practices conservative elements that date back to the precontact period, Maya religion is extremely fluid in the way oral traditions often are. Religious symbols, like all symbols and meanings, are subject to change and reinterpretation, but religious symbols seem to be especially open to creative and dynamic reinterpretations. This is perhaps due to the nature of the symbology not kept in check by material constraints and realities but rather more open to play. Think of the children's game "telephone," where one person whispers a statement in another's ear and it goes around a group, coming out very differently. Talking to individuals about traditional beliefs elicits a wide range of opinion, making it difficult to tease out clear patterns. At the same time there are common themes, a few leitmotifs.

People claim to recover from physical ailments after Maya healing ceremonies. Very often the diagnosis involves uncovering interpersonal conflict, and the prescribed cure usually involves resolving these conflicts, practically and spiritually. Ill will—either directed at another or directed toward one's self—can damage one's health and welfare. Rituals are also prescribed, and for sacrifices—depending on the illness and its severity and also on the personal resources of the person being treated—a greater payment is required for a proportionately greater outcome. There is normally a fee based on the items needed for the ceremony, and it is customary to give the *aj q'ij* an honorarium in cash. The most honest and respected *aj q'ijab'* do not ask for a specific payment but rather let people pay as they see fit and as they are able. Many others ask for a specific fee based on the services provided, and they have a set amount that they ask for. Most religious specialists maintain their own *milpas*, and many have other jobs as well. Some are very successful. One *aj q'ij* owns a local transportation company and lives in one of the finest houses in town. Another is a very poor man, growing enough corn for his family to eat throughout the year and making ends meet by working odd jobs around town.

Women religious specialists are rare but not unheard of in traditional Maya religion. Most women day-keepers report that they, like their male colleagues, were called to this work and not really given a choice. Paula is a university-educated, rather progressive Maya woman, who is also a day-keeper, like her husband. Paula is aware of what many people say about Maya religion (that it is idolatry and witchcraft). But she argues that these conceptions are based on erroneous ideas. It is not true, she says, that Maya religion worships many gods. There are many aspects of a singular god and a pronounced reverence toward the natural elements. Thus one might pray to God before cutting down a tree, explaining that the tree was being cut out of need, not just for pleasure or fun, and ask forgiveness. This is not praying to the tree or a god of nature, but rather praying to a unified God in its aspect as protector of the natural world. Paula is a strong advocate of religious tolerance, seeing sectarianism as a bad influence that is dividing Maya communities. She explains that one must be called to be a Maya priest; it is not something that one just decides to do. Indeed there are fundamental predispositions, and even the shape of an infant's placenta may foretell a calling as an *aj q'ij*. She tells of a ceremony she once attended at which she threw some candles into the fire, but they flew in the opposite direction. The *aj q'ij* presiding over the ceremony explained that she had an unpaid debt. In fact, a man to whom she used to take cigarettes had just died before she could bring him the last ones, so she prayed for forgiveness and gave an offering. She also says that she has seen a Maya priest materialize a dead person in the air at a funeral (an event she tries to explain with a hypothesis involving subatomic fluidity).

The idea that Maya religion is not polytheistic is frequently expressed by its practitioners, who explain that there are but various aspects of a single deity. Maya religion also has a significant dose of fatalism in terms of preordained destiny, but this tendency is tempered by a belief in the possibility of change, specifically directed change. On the one hand, humans are not always able to predict or influence events; gods may act maliciously. What tempers their anger is tribute, homage, prayer, sacrifice, and offerings. Humans are obligated to respect their creators, the gods and ancestors. As long as they maintain this covenant, the cyclic cosmic forces that animate the universe will continue, the seasons will progress.

Maya ceremonies take place in several different types of places. Often they are conducted in the hills, at altars built on top of ancient ruins, places that are considered to be especially powerful. These sites are ranked in importance. Especially important ceremonies are preferably conducted at places where a great deal of energy is concentrated (e.g., caves or ancient sites such as Iximche'). Ceremonies are also conducted in *milpas*, in open air patios, and in rooms of a house; some medical and midwifery ceremonies are conducted in sweat baths. Maya homes often have one or more small altars. With their candles, flowers, and images of Jesus or the Virgin Mary, many of these would be seen by their owners as strictly Catholic in nature (and similar to ones found in *ladino* homes). However, others would include Maya artifacts that a family may have found in their *milpa*, used to invoke the Maya past and ancestors.

For ceremonies, the floor of the room with the altar is usually covered with fresh pine needles, giving the room an almost overwhelming aroma of pine. Fire is an important element of Maya ceremonies, and a fire must be built to consume the offerings given. These offerings may include incense, liquor, candles, sugar, and other flammable items. When they are burned their essence rises into the sky to serve as an offering to the gods, adding another layer of soot to already black ceilings when conducted indoors. Corn is also a common offering, as are animals at certain important ceremonies. Chickens are the most common offerings, although goats are sometimes sacrificed. The blood of animal sacrifices is drained into a hole with offerings, and the meat is then usually consumed as part of a ritual meal.

Lying just under the surface of many of these issues of Maya belief is the idea that Maya identity is not something that one can deny or shake off. It is tied not so much to clothes and language as to heritage and descent as well as a way of being and acting in the world. It brings with it a sense of destiny, but mutable destiny that must be reconciled with individual desires. Older Kaqchikeles often speak of the obligation young people owe to their ancestors, an obligation that should be repaid through respect and filial piety. For young Kaqchikeles some of the duties that go along with being Maya seem to thwart their desire to be progressive and modern. And synthesizing such competing intentions drives the dynamism of Kaqchikel culture.

BELIEF AND INTERGENERATIONAL CHANGE

Margarita, a woman in her mid-forties, comes from a respected local family, one whose surname frequently pops up in colonial documents. She is a midwife, one of the most traditional Maya professions, while at the same time she is a registered nurse, working in the town's public health center. She also runs a small pharmacy in the front of her house, selling a few prescription drugs and administering injections.

Margarita charges 20 quetzales (about $3.25) for prenatal sweatbath therapy sessions, and she generally does fewer than other midwives. In the countryside, midwives generally charge about 3 quetzales per sweatbath, and other midwives in urban Tecpán charge about 10 quetzales per session. Margarita feels justified in charging substantially more than her competition primarily because she is also a nurse and often combines examinations in the health center with traditional sweatbath therapies. Her husband and four daughters take a mixed view of her work as a midwife. They appreciate the importance of her work, of bringing new life into the world, and yet they cannot help but resent the great demands it makes on family life. There is a salient ideal among many Kaqchikeles that women should dedicate themselves completely to their families, and regular jobs outside of the house (although sometimes necessary) are frowned upon. But the work of a midwife takes Margarita away from her family at all hours; she is often not there to supervise meal preparation or even put the kids to bed. Her plight is not uncommon, and midwives frequently report that their work engenders family disputes.

Margarita sees midwifery as her destiny, an obligation she cannot shirk. She tells the story of the time she was attending a woman in a sweatbath and began to smell something burning. She asked her patient if she was burning incense and she said no, but they then both saw wisps of smoke appear over the coals. In the midst of the sweatbath therapy, the patient passed out and Margarita could not revive her; Margarita called out for help and the woman's mother came out and they carried the patient to a bed. Margarita then went back into the sweatbath and began to pray fervently: "Grandmothers, Grandfathers, tell me what I am doing wrong, tell me if this is not my calling, let me know before an innocent person dies." Suddenly a beam of light appeared through a small hole in the roof, illuminating the face of a woman that looked like an ancient Maya portrait. The woman spoke and told Margarita that she should drink tortilla water (a mixture of hot water and broken up corn tortillas), a crucial part of the sweatbath ceremony that Margarita had overlooked. She did so, and the woman regained consciousness and was fine. When

Margarita got home, she found her legs covered in bruises, and her mother explained that she had been made hot by the ancestors as punishment for not performing ceremonies correctly. Since that incident, Margarita has been careful not to be hurried in her duties and not to neglect any of the ceremonial obligations of a midwife, even if this means being away from home longer.

Margarita's oldest daughter, María, is particularly perturbed at her mother's absences. One night they were supposed to have dinner at a friend's house, and they were running late because Margarita was attending a birth. After she delivered the baby she had to burn the placenta, but when she got home she realized that she was out of wood and had to run down the street to a neighbor who sells firewood. As her mother sat in the patio trying to start a fire and battling the wind and drizzle, María became increasingly frustrated about their tardiness. For María, a young woman much concerned with being progressive, modern, and thus punctual, this was inexcusable behavior. As the clock ticked further away from the appointed hour, María began scolding her mother, saying that she should not be so concerned with the welfare of her patients and especially should cut short these antiquated customs, such as burning the placenta. (Why not just throw it away in the trash like they do at the hospital?) In her frustration over her mother's seeming stubbornness, María ran toward the door, tripped, and seriously twisted her ankle. She had to be taken to the regional hospital, where x-rays found no broken bones, but so severe was the strain that she had to use crutches to walk for several weeks.

In the traditional Maya calendar, the day that María twisted her ankle was 8 Ajmaq'. Her mother explains that this is a day for paying for one's sins, a clear sign of her daughter's waywardness. The proximate cause for this accident was the fight over being late to the dinner, precipitated by her mother burning the placenta of a birth she had attended, a central part of her obligation as a midwife. The larger cause, however, was María's incomplete acceptance of her cultural heritage and disregard for her mother's customs. María has always walked an uneasy line between *ladino* and Indian culture, and she says she feels more comfortable in Western-style clothes than in traditional *traje*. Her family explicitly attributes a long string of mishaps that have befallen María over the last few years to this incomplete acceptance of her ethnic identity. They view her Maya-ness as something inherent, ingrained, and to a degree immutable. For María to try to resist her fate of being Maya leads to a state of metaphysical imbalance that affects the way in which she interacts with the world.

A similar case involved Ana, a young woman in her teens and a member of a prosperous Tecpán family. Her father, Miguel, in his mid- to late-forties, has long been a staunch proponent of Catholicism and progress. His family says that for a time he even made his wife and daughters wear Western dress rather than *traje*, and he encouraged speaking Spanish. Positioning himself as a progressive and upwardly mobile man—a Guatemalan as much, or more, than an Indian—he was known for taking a dim view of traditional Maya culture. But during her last year in high school, his daughter, Ana, came down with severe arthritis in her knees. It was said that the illness was brought on by the girl washing her school uniform, not letting it dry sufficiently, and then wearing it the next day to classes. The pain got so bad at one point that she could not even walk, having to be carried from her bed to the bathroom. The family took her to doctors in Tecpán and then to the departmental capital, Chimaltenango, for tests and to see specialists. Various medicines were prescribed, and they temporarily took away the pain, but not for long. One day, a friend told them that there would be a Maya ceremony at Iximché, a celebration of the fifth anniversary of the pro-Maya radio program Mayab' Winäq, and encouraged them to take Ana to see the many Maya priests who would be in attendance. But Ana resisted the idea, having been brought up in a strict Catholic household and not believing in the *brujería* ("witchcraft") of Maya ceremonies. She firmly refused to go, and her parents decided not to pressure her into doing something that she was so opposed to. On the day of the ceremony they had an appointment with a doctor in Chimaltenango, and on the way home they saw the truck carrying the marimba and the people from Mayab' Winäq, with posters advertising the fiesta. Ana saw the truck and said it looked like it might be fun. And so they went. At the end of the ceremony the *aj q'ij* (a woman from a neighboring community) prayed over Ana, and Ana was feeling better by the time they got home. The *aj q'ij* offered to come by the next day to perform another ceremony, which she did, and a few days later they performed a final ceremony at Iximché again. At the end of the ceremonies, Ana was cured and her father convinced of the power of traditional Maya religion.

CATHOLICISM

Although the majority of Tecpanecos consider themselves Catholic, Catholicism in Tecpán (as elsewhere) encompasses a great deal of diversity. On the one hand, a generally conservative doctrine is espoused from the pulpit of the main church; sermons routinely denounce contraceptive use, extramarital sexuality, idolatry in the form of traditionalist Maya religion, and other such prohibited behaviors. On the other hand, Tecpán is also home to a number of offshoot *congregaciones* with their own interpretations of what it means to be a good Catholic. Ultimately, as with all religions, beliefs and symbolic meanings vary significantly from individual to individual, as each interprets the precepts of received doctrine through the lens of personal experience.

The main Catholic church in Tecpán, restored after the 1976 earthquake, rises impressively over the town hall, the municipal market building, and a small park off the main square (see Figure 5.1). Its large wooden doors remain open throughout the day, providing entry to the dim, cool sanctuary, which is about the length of a football field and as tall as a multistory building. Throughout the day, a steady stream of people come to pray and meditate in the pews or light a candle in front of one of the saints' images that line the walls: women on their

Figure 5.1 The Catholic
church in Tecpán.

way to market with children in tow, men stopping by to say a prayer before they make a request to the municipality, adolescents offering their personal burdens. There is a regular morning mass and several larger services on Thursdays (market day) and Sundays. During mass, babies cry, kids run around the pews, and people drift in and out of the sanctuary; so, even though the majority of the congregation stays in their pews for the whole service, the feel is much more fluid and vibrant than the staid norm of a mass in the United States.

Two priests preside over the church in Tecpán. The senior padre is a *ladino* man in his mid-forties, and his assistant is a younger Kaqchikel priest from the neighboring town of Patzún. Their different styles reflect the multifaceted nature of the Guatemalan Church, simultaneously conservative and liberal. The senior priest speaks of developing Tecpán—weaning it from a dependence on subsistence agriculture—and he sees the church as providing crucial support for this grander project by instilling a sense of discipline among the faithful. Many Catholic Tecpanecos see this as the right and proper role of a parish priest minding his flock. Others chafe at what they see as gratuitous exercises of power in approving marriages, confirmations, and other church rites. The younger priest appears more open to adapting the church to local needs rather than vice versa. He occasionally delivers services in Kaqchikel and cultivates relations with youth groups and adult organizations based out of the church. The church runs two schools (a private grade school and a pre-seminary), and through these and other outreach programs it has allowed a significant number of Tecpaneco youths (Indian and *ladino*) to realize goals that they might never have conceived possible otherwise. Many Kaqchikel professionals from Tecpán trace their career trajectories back to formative experiences that somehow involve the church.

The most progressive elements within Tecpán's Catholic Church have formed a number of *congregaciones*, groups that operate under the umbrella of the main parish and sponsor additional services. *Congregación* membership varies from as few as five or ten to as many as a hundred individuals, and the larger *congregaciones* have built their own meeting halls. Each *congregación* has developed its own variation and points of emphasis within Catholic doctrine. A few are charismatic, with services filled with music, dancing, and audience participation, not unlike many Evangelical Protestant services; one focuses on improving family relationships through study group services; and another is made up exclusively of women and addresses women's issues. *Congregación* members often speak of their spirituality in therapeutic terms—for example, how the *congregación* has helped them overcome (or at least come to terms with) personal problems. Although the vocabulary is different, such views allude to paradigms of groundedness and centeredness discussed previously.

In addition to *congregaciones*, Tecpán supports a number of *cofradías*, hierarchically organized religious brotherhoods devoted to the veneration of a particular saint. Although the institution was brought over by the Spaniards, *cofradías* have long been integrated into Maya social organization and are considered by many as emblematic of hybrid Maya-Catholic practices. Reportedly strong just thirty or forty years ago, these semi-independent groups operating under the auspices of the parish have lost much of their former importance. However, in comparison to the early 1980s, there has been a revitalization of interest, including a growing number of younger members and a reappearance of men's *cofradía* dress (a wool poncho dyed with blue indigo). In the late 1990s Tecpán had eight active *cofradías*, the most important of which was the *cofradía* associated with the town's patron saint (Saint Francis of Assisi). Most members of the San Francisco *cofradía* came from *aldeas*, although they rented space in the town proper to house their saint's image and ceremonial paraphernalia (see Figure 5.2).

Among more traditionalist Tecpanecos, *cofradías* are important arenas of social practice, implicating individual views of the self and the collectivity. On the one hand, *cofradías* stress the common good over individual self-interest; the duties (*cargos*) of members are carried out at a sacrifice for the benefit of all. On the other hand, social prestige is explicitly acknowledged in the *cofradía* hierarchy.

Figure 5.2   Members of the cofradía *and their wives carry an image of San Francisco de Assisi, Tecpán's patron saint.*

The senior *cofradía* official is called *Tetata* (or *Cofrade*), and under his direction are four *mayordomos*, each with his own specific *cargos*. The *Tetata* is in charge of organizing all *cofradía* functions, maintaining contact with the priest, and ensuring the financial stability of the group. The *mayordomo* positions are ranked, with each post carrying specific duties. The First *Mayordomo* holds the keys to the *cofre* (the chest that holds ritual paraphernalia and clothing for the statues). The Second *Mayordomo* keeps the saints' images clean and makes sure fresh flowers are always at their feet. The Third *Mayordomo* is supposed to sweep the church, and the Fourth *Mayordomo* serves as the personal aide to the *Tetata*. The wife of the *Cofrade* and the wives of the *mayordomos* form a parallel structure, called simply *texela* (the women). The *texela* also have certain prescribed duties, including taking incense to the saint's images, preparing meals for *cofradía* functions, and making new clothes for the saint's images. The wife of the *Tetata* directs these activities. In addition there is a parallel set of five couples (*säkalej*) paired with the couples of the *cofradía* proper. Their job is to aid the member couples in carrying out their tasks, and the position of these auxiliary posts is at the bottom of the *cofradía* hierarchy.

The importance of the *cofradía* in the social life of Mesoamerican Indian communities has been well documented. Eric Wolf (1957) saw the prevalence of *cofradías* and the cargo system as mechanisms for maintaining the inward focus of "closed corporate peasant communities." This idea, later elaborated by Waldemar Smith (1977) and George Foster (1965), viewed Indian communities as having developed as mechanisms to maintain economic and social isolation from national systems and to redistribute wealth within communities. Wolf (1986) and others have come to question the validity of this concept as it has been widely applied to modern Indian communities, which are enmeshed in national and international political and economic systems. Regardless of the *cofradías'* role in the past, it is undeniable that the *cofradía* system has eroded significantly, and its future is uncertain. With little interest among the under-thirty population, *cofradías* seem doomed to die out with the current generation of older adherents. Economic factors are most often cited as the cause of their decline. Membership is expensive, and many younger Indians, striving for upward mobility, are unwilling to pay the costs.

Even though the percentage of Tecpanecos who identify themselves as Catholic decreased dramatically in the latter part of the twentieth century, the Church continues to play an important role in Tecpán life. Church tradition provides moral guideposts for many Tecpanecos. At the same time, that tradition is actively redefined—made meaningful in new ways that respond to changing contingencies—by *congregaciones*, *cofradías*, and individual paths to spiritual fulfillment.

PROTESTANTISM

The words pierced the early morning darkness. "Arise! Arise! And accept Jesus Christ as your savior." They emanated from a jeep with a loudspeaker attached to its roof that was being driven through the streets of Tecpán by two Protestant missionaries from the United States. The foreigners were members of an evangelical congregation back home who were visiting sister churches in Guatemala in 1980 and distributing inspirational tracts, calendars with illustrations of Bible stories, and Spanish editions of the New Testament. While it was (and continues to be) quite common to hear municipal, religious, and commercial announcements blaring from loudspeakers mounted on vehicles or church sermons from loudspeakers nailed on church roofs, the early morning hour—about 4:00 A.M.—marked this effort as noteworthy and suggested an innovation in the competition for Tecpanecos' hearts and souls.

The cross-cultural traffic in religious ideas has a long history in this area of the world (one could argue it dates from well before the arrival of the Spanish with Catholicism); however, Protestantism is a fairly recent addition to the blend.

Although Protestants—generally British—entered the Spanish/Catholic landscape of colonial Guatemala on occasion, it was only toward the end of the nineteenth century, after the country had gained its independence, that the legal dissemination and practice of Protestantism became possible. In 1873, President Justo Rufino Barrios introduced a Freedom of Worship decree that stripped Catholicism of its status as state religion and allowed for the establishment of Protestant communities of worship (Garrard-Burnett 1998: 11). In Tecpán, Protestant churches appeared in the early twentieth century. For example, in her detailed work on Protestantism in Guatemala, Virginia Garrard-Burnett notes a case from 1947 in which "independent evangelicals in three churches—in Guatemala City, Escuintla, and Tecpán—became Southern Baptists" (1998: 86). The independent evangelicals mentioned here had earlier split from the Central America Mission, a missionary agency founded in the United States in 1888 and active in Guatemala for over a hundred years, because of financial issues. They joined with the Southern Baptists because of affinities to the Baptists' positions on doctrine and baptism (Garrard-Burnett 1998: 24, 86).

Issues such as these—financial and doctrinal, as well as social, economic, political, and natural—help to define the conversions and rapid growth of Protestantism in Guatemala in general and Tecpán specifically. However, two assumptions that are often made must be challenged to understand the impact of Protestantism in this country. First, although missionaries from the United States have played an enormous role in establishing Protestantism in Guatemala, this does not mean that the beliefs and practices of the foreigners have been accepted "whole cloth." Within limits, Tecpanecos—and every other missionized people—remake what is given them to suit their own purposes and their larger conceptual world. This will become clearer with examples. And second, although the presidency of Efraín Ríos Montt, the born-again Christian who assumed leadership after a 1982 coup, is often thought to mark the start of the sharp rise in Guatemalan Protestantism, this is not really true. The roots of the increase lie in the postrevolutionary period of the 1960s and got another boost during the aftermath of the 1976 earthquake. What characterizes all of these moments and what can help explain people's conversions to different forms of Protestantism are the "tectonic social shifts" (Garrard-Burnett 1998: 119) of the second half of the twentieth century, including the increased military presence and violence of the civil war; waves of economic hardship; population growth and land pressures; and, in the case of the earthquake, the complete destruction of the town and death of 3,000 Tecpanecos. Hardships, tensions, and calamities such as these, reflected in large and small ways in daily life, push people to return to core questions having to do with senses of self, family, and community life.

Protestant groups in Tecpán number in the dozens and include the Church of God, Assembly of God, Príncipe de Paz, Filadelfia, Agape, Bethesda, and Monte de Oliva. These range from the large "formal" churches such as Bethesda (with its own primary school) to tiny breakaway congregations formed by a handful of people who have turned from the teachings of a church to create one that better meets their own needs and predilections. Despite the relatively large number of churches and the frequent appearance of new ones, an outside observer can get a sense that a finite number of issues—elaborated on within a particular church in formal beliefs and practices—are embraced, rejected, combined, or elaborated on so as to distinguish one institution from another. These also relate in important ways to how people define themselves, value life, and place themselves within a religious cosmos.

In a very general sense, and based on dozens of conversations with Tecpanecos over the years, Protestant teachings center around questions of community, moral and spiritual orientation, and relationship to the sacred. A person is said to have a soul or spirit, although individuals speak more often of putting themselves in God's hands, surrendering themselves to God's Spirit, or allowing the Holy Spirit to enter them. The latter can manifest itself publicly by speaking in tongues or a healing experience in which the person claims to have ceded himself or herself to God and been cured. On the other hand, people who do not put their faith in the divine may be plagued by ill health, vices, or other temptations or, in general, exhibit moral degradation.

Members of Protestant churches also point to the quality of the religious experience created within a service and by their fellow members. Some services are characterized and valued by some as being solemn and respectful, which believers see as honoring God. Others favor services that are *más alegre* ("more cheerful"), with music, clapping, and praiseful shouting, which are seen as rousing people to religious passion. In no case do the Protestant spaces include icons, which are associated with Catholicism.

In contrast to Catholics, Protestant leaders may arrive at their religious calling not through study but rather through a *don* ("gift") for preaching. This may be revealed to them through intense participation in services where they are entered by the Holy Spirit or on occasion through dreams. In some ways this is not unlike the experiences reported by traditional religious specialists, for example midwives speaking of their callings.

These last couple of examples point to the ways that individuals define themselves by what they are not. Within the community of Protestant churches, individuals can specify in great detail how their beliefs and practices differ from those of other Protestant sects. In addition, an important part of being Protestant in Tecpán is not being Catholic or following the ways of traditional Maya customs labeled *brujería*. Catholics and Maya traditionalists alike take a liberal view of tobacco and alcohol consumption; in fact, drinking and smoking are often key elements of their rituals. In contrast, Protestants vehemently proscribe the use of alcohol, tobacco, and often even dancing.

Although the boundaries between Protestant, Catholic, and traditionalist Maya belief may seem absolute, in practice they are actually quite permeable. In one Tecpán family, second-generation Protestants, the mother and young son once suffered a serious attack of *susto*. Their church provided a general sense of comfort, but for a specific remedy they turned to an elderly relative who could prescribe a traditional medicinal remedy: sweeping the site of transgression with a branch from a specific bush. In addition, the young boy was given several doses of a popular tonic aimed at calming nerves. This is a family that would be loathe to attend a Maya ritual or pay for the services of an *aj q'ij*, and yet in this case they did not hesitate to draw upon their heritage for a type of spiritual healing.

THE *K'U'X* OF DARKNESS AND BEYOND

In dealing with Kaqchikel hearts, souls, bodies, and beliefs, we have tried to show the complex and overlapping nature of the concepts and issues. However, it is easy to overlook the even larger contexts in which these conceptions are being formulated. For example, Kaqchikel soul concepts are not so far removed from Guatemalan politics and global economics. The violence, for example, indelibly shaped the form of Kaqchikel souls, just as it did many other aspects of Tecpán life. In this way *la violencia* is certainly comparable to the effects of the Holocaust on European Jews: Life can never be the same again once one has first-hand knowledge and memory of the depths of the human condition. It is a knowledge that affects individual psyches and all social relations. Linda Green (1999), in a study of Kaqchikel war widows, reports that these women often complain of chronic illnesses associated with the *k'u'x*: heartache, nerves (*nervios*), fright (*susto*). But they have also found collective strength in sharing their common condition and have worked actively to reestablish some semblance of the social bonds that kept them grounded and centered in pre-*violencia* times.

As discussed in Chapter 7, new economic conditions in the Tecpán area have likewise affected what is considered to be soulful expression and appropriate behavior. This knowledge helps us move toward seeing Kaqchikel thought and behavior as an ever-emergent construction, constrained by psychological predispositions and cultural norms as well as national politics and global markets.

Further Reading

Garrard-Burnett, Virginia. 1998. *Protestantism in Guatemala*. Austin: University of Texas Press.

Smith, Waldemar. 1977. *The fiesta system and economic change*. New York: Columbia University Press.

Stoll, David. 1990. *Is Latin America turning Protestant?: The politics of evangelical growth*. Berkeley: University of California Press.

Warren, Kay. 1978. *The symbolism of subordination: Indian identity in a Guatemalan town*. Austin: University of Texas Press.

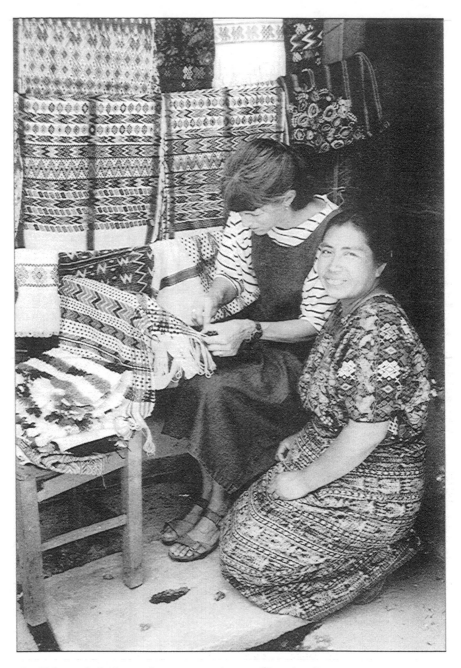

Carol helps put the finishing touches on a weaving by tying off loose threads.

6

Language, Dress, and Identity

Ethnicity must be marked somehow. If people are to make distinctions between "them" and "us," they need to recognize differences, find them meaningful, make them explicit, and employ them regularly in a wide range of circumstances. Anthropologist Pierre van den Berghe (1981), who has done extensive fieldwork in Maya communities, writes that certain markers of ethnicity are better than others because they appear more authentic or natural, and that the best markers, in terms of accuracy, are those that are readily identifiable and yet not readily or willingly assumed. Primary among potential candidates are language and dress, although phenotype, religion, surnames, or any number of other markers may also be used. For example, most adults can't easily pick up a new language. Languages are generally learned from birth, and if a person learns a language too late in life the accent or errors in speech can mark him or her as "non-native." Thus, language can indicate the cultural authenticity or nativeness of the person using it.

Clothing might seem more malleable—objects that anyone could put on—and, indeed, in a certain sense this is true. However, people speak of clothing as if it were their second skin: something in which they feel comfortable physically and psychologically, which they see as a true public representation of their selves, and which they do not in fact change easily (except perhaps as a costume or disguise). Like language, it is a very public marker, and people who are inconsistent in their dress (whatever that means locally) may be eyed suspiciously.

It would be a mistake, however, to consider such markers of ethnic identity too rigidly, as they are dynamic objects, constantly defined and redefined through experience. They are the tools through which ethnicity is negotiated and exhibited, and their power comes in part from their multiple uses and symbolic malleability. Like all signs, they are simultaneously form (perceived as visible, audible, etc.) and concept, with meanings understood by the collectivity but innovated on and manipulated by individuals.

Beyond the idea that people of a particular group regularly or generally use, say, a particular language or style of dress, what more is meant by the claim that something is an "ethnic marker?" Along with the notion of the current use of markers within a group, ethnicity has to do with a sense of cultural heritage. Emblems of ethnic identity proclaim that this is a group with a history and that history informs who these people are. Ethnicity also implies a common origin, no matter how distant, which in turn implies some sort of biological relatedness. The catch, of course, is that ideas of relatedness are putative and selectively pronounced, and given the right conditions there is a great deal of flexibility in ascribing ethnicity. This was evident in the 2000 U.S. census, which showed a rapid increase during the 1990s of individuals who identified themselves as Native American, a much greater increase than population growth itself could account for. Likewise there has long existed the possibility in Guatemala of native Maya "passing" as *ladinos*, which often involves a person's refraining from speaking a Mayan language or abandoning the use of Maya dress. These examples show the constructed nature of ethnic ascription as being not so much the result of biological heritage as of cultural construction. With this in mind, we turn to an examination of language and dress, perhaps the preeminent public markers of Maya identity.

KAQCHIKEL LANGUAGE AND CULTURE

Tecpán has been a work site for a number of Peace Corps volunteers over the decades and, during the early 1980s, was deemed "safe" longer than many other central highland communities. In time, however, it too had to be abandoned as a site, until 1994, when the Peace Corps once again assigned a volunteer to Tecpán. He was a sincere and eager young man, but he was plagued by the language barrier. After a couple of months of intensive Spanish classes, he could more or less get his point across in that language, but he found that most of the farmers he needed to talk with spoke Kaqchikel. Once, after a meeting of a farmers' cooperative in an outlying village, he returned to town totally frustrated: "They're just speaking in Kaqchikel to piss me off," he complained. And so it must feel to many outsiders who visit the highlands. Of course it was presumptuous of the Peace Corps volunteer to expect the whole group to switch to an uncomfortable language just to accommodate him. At the same time, using Kaqchikel can often be a subtle means of exercising power. Very few non-Maya speak the language, so it offers an effective means of public yet hidden communication. It is a way for individuals to talk among themselves without being understood by outsiders, unless, of course, that "outsider" is another speaker of the Kaqchikel language.

In lists of traits that purportedly distinguish the Maya as a culture group, language is invariably emphasized. Victoria Bricker (n.d.) has observed that it is really only language affinity that clearly sets off the Maya from their indigenous neighbors in Mesoamerica. The Maya are often represented as ethno-linguistic

Language Change and Diversity

In 1945, the Yiddish linguist Max Weinreich noted that a language is but a dialect with an army; that is to say, that language designations are as much political as scientific. Indeed language boundaries are always somewhat arbitrarily drawn, with an eye toward political expediency as much as scientific exactitude. Inculcated notions of rigid political borders reinforce views of linguistic boundedness: In France they speak French, in Germany they speak German. But even in this seemingly clear-cut example, the dichotomy breaks down: Not only does contemporary German include a large number of loan words from French, but people living in the border regions speak a combination of the two. In mapping language frontiers, linguists must rely on arbitrary cut-off points—couched in the hard statistics of proportions of shared words and grammatical forms—to determine where one language ends and another begins. Thus, in Guatemala, there are either twenty or twenty-one Mayan languages spoken, depending on whether one considers Achi a dialect of K'iche' or an independent language (an issue that has sparked heated debate among Maya linguists and activists). Similar problems arise in trying to date the chronological development of contemporary Mayan languages, which are understood to have evolved over the millennia from a single language that linguists have named "Proto-Mayan." Historical linguists compare word lists from Mayan languages and calculate the degree of divergence between each. Then, using a conventional scale of the rate of language change, they are able to calculate approximate dates for language splits. It is important to keep in mind, however, that language change is a gradual process, and mutual intelligibility is lost only over very long periods of time.

groups: the Kaqchikeles, who speak Kaqchikel; the K'iche', who speak K'iche'; and so on. More broadly, Maya peoples speak one of thirty related Mayan languages in southern Mexico, Belize, Guatemala, and Honduras (not to mention their occasional use in immigrant communities worldwide). These are all part of the Mayan family of Mesoamerican languages, which once extended into El Salvador as well and included languages that are now extinct (see box). (Note the linguistic convention that has developed in Mesoamerican studies: The term "Mayan" is generally used with languages, while "Maya" is preferred in other contexts.)

The native language of Tecpán and the surrounding region is Kaqchikel, which is part of the K'iche'an branch of the Mayan language family: Kaqchikel likely split off from other K'iche'an languages about 900 years ago. As with

Spanish and Portuguese, there is a good deal of mutual intelligibility between Kaqchikel and its most closely related languages, Tz'utujil and K'iche', and Achi'. Good-willed speakers of these different languages can generally get their point across—whether speaking to each other in the marketplace or in conversation on a bus—although the nuances of discourse are easily lost. In addition, Kaqchikel, like most Mayan languages, has pronounced regional and local dialects. Native speakers can generally identify another person's hometown by his or her dialect, and certain dialects enjoy greater social prestige because of their association with affluent towns or because of their perceived linguistic purity. Dialectical differences are sometimes comical, good for provoking laughter when people from different communities get together. For example, in the Kaqchikel dialect of Patzún *kachuk'e* means "sit down," while in Tecpán it means "mount," with a vague sexual connotation.

The phonology, or system of meaningful sounds, for the Kaqchikel language, is significantly different from that of Indo-European languages. Recent neuropsychological work has shown that a person's basic phonological pattern is laid down in the first ten years of life, and sounds that are not introduced in these first ten years are rarely ever fully mastered. Thus, for example, the use of glottal stops found in Kaqchikel is difficult for the person raised monolingually in Spanish or English. Glottal stops are produced by rapidly constricting the air opening in the back of the throat to suddenly stop all air (and thus sound) from escaping. Glottal stops may follow either consonants or vowels. There are a few examples of glottal stops used by English speakers, such as in "uh oh." After "uh" most American English speakers constrict the back of the throat to produce a glottal stop. The most difficult glottals in Kaqchikel are the consonants q' and k'; pronouncing these is something like trying to swallow the back of one's tongue. (Samples of Kaqchikel phonemes and speech are available at this book's website.) Kaqchikel, like many Mayan languages, also has an ergative pronoun structure, which is another challenge for speakers of Indo-European languages. In ergative languages, the direct object pronouns used with transitive verbs become subject pronouns when used with intransitive verbs, while a separate set of pronouns serves as the subject of transitive verbs. "Translating" this into English, a person would use a direct object pronoun such as "me" or "him" (e.g., "She saw me" or "I saw him") as the subject pronoun of sentences with intransitive verbs (e.g., "Me sleep" or "Him sleep"). What this means for everyday linguistic interactions is that a Tecpaneco—Indian or *ladino*—who has been raised from birth speaking only Spanish can find it difficult to master Kaqchikel later in life and might end up sounding less than "native."

As anyone who has had classroom language training knows, competence in the basic phonology and grammar of a language hardly makes a person fully functional. The Kaqchikel Mayan used in many contexts is excruciatingly subtle, formal, and context-sensitive and takes years to master. Kaqchikeles place a high value on oratory skills, which involve the ability to influence the opinions of oth-

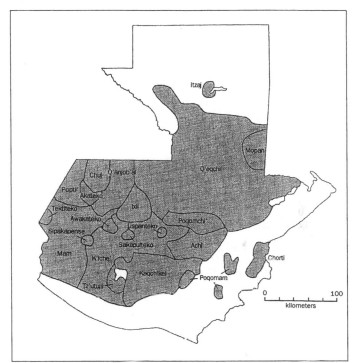

Figure 6.1 The Mayan languages of Guatemala.

ers (so crucial in Maya models of consensus decision-making), while at the same time valuing subtlety of expression, skill in punning and metaphorical constructions, and a formal roteness that some may confuse with an evasion of pressing underlying issues. This formality in Kaqchikel discourse, however, also provides strict ground rules that encourage subtle forms of creativity of expression. Mastering these speech forms is a goal of some young Indians involved in revitalization efforts. For them an ability to speak Kaqchikel eloquently in sacred *and* secular ritual contexts marks not only a cultural genealogy descending from their ancestors but also the vitality of the language itself (and metanymically all of Maya culture) as well as their own participation in the Maya movement.

Speaking Kaqchikel Mayan is one thing that regularly sets Tecpanecos Indians apart from *ladinos*, especially among adults. A handful of ladinos in town can understand the gist of conversations in Kaqchikel and may even speak a few words (if they aren't too embarrassed to be heard doing so in public), but for the most part *ladinos* have very little interest in learning the language. A complaint voiced by some Kaqchikel speakers is that *ladinos* do not even know how to say *matyox* ("thank you") in the language spoken by the majority population in town. Spanish is the language of government and courts, is used for the vast majority of school instruction, and is the language of big business.

Speaking Kaqchikel, or even speaking Spanish with a particular accent, clearly marks a person as "Indian" and calls up all of the prejudices and stereotypes that go along with that designation. In fact, there is a widespread belief among *ladinos*, and some Indians, that Kaqchikel (and other Mayan languages) are innately inferior to Spanish; they refer to the different Mayan languages as dialects (*dialectos*) rather than languages (*idiomas*) comparable to Spanish and English. Supposed proof of the inadequacies of Mayan languages comes from the many Spanish loanwords found in the basic vocabulary (including numbers and a large number of legal and technical terms). If they are adequate languages, the argument goes, then why do they need terms from Spanish? From a linguistic perspective such critiques are baseless, for all languages borrow words. Spanish, for instance, has a large number of loan words from Arabic, a relic of the 500 years of Moorish occupation of the Iberian Peninsula.

Theories and memories of language acquisition, as well as assessments of the social worth of different languages, abound in Tecpán and shape people's attitudes and actions. Some Kaqchikeles believe that the ability to speak a language is somehow instinctual and that their children will learn Kaqchikel without explicit attention to the matter. Many older Kaqchikel adults vividly recall the trauma of being forced to learn Spanish in school, where teachers would often mock and hit children for speaking their native language. And now English competes with Kaqchikel for the attention and interest of Maya students monolingual in Spanish who claim that, when it comes to making the effort to learn another language, "English is more useful" for their aspirations in life. As a result, there are increasing numbers of Maya children who are not learning Kaqchikel at home, their parents consciously speaking to them only in Spanish so that they do not suffer the discrimination that they endured and so that they have the linguistic ability to succeed in the modern world. This means many of these young Kaqchikeles have not picked up the native language of their parents and/or grandparents; even when they have very good comprehension they may be unable (or unwilling) to speak in Kaqchikel and instead resort to Spanish. These sorts of language attitudes and actions help make sense of statistics collected by Ted in 1994 showing 62 percent of respondents in Tecpán claiming very good or average fluency in Kaqchikel, while 38 percent claim little or no proficiency at all. Although comparable statistics don't exist for earlier eras, we feel confident in stating that the percentage of the population fluent in Kaqchikel was higher when today's parents and grandparents were children.

For some—principally the people with a strong sentiment toward and speaking ability in Kaqchikel—this shift away from speaking a Mayan language maps into an unwelcome change in the behavior of children. These people see inherent in a child's ability to speak Kaqchikel not so much a mastery of grammar and vocabulary (parents rarely speak in these terms) but rather a way to express key cultural values by means of the appropriate use of language. Thus, it is not uncommon to hear a child address an older woman and say "Takaya' numak, Nana." ("Excuse me for asking, Mother.") Such expressions of deference are forms of respect that encap-

The Linguistic Relativity Hypothesis

The linguistic relativity hypothesis (frequently and, to some, misleadingly labeled the Sapir-Whorf Hypothesis [Duranti 2001: 216–218]) proposes that linguistic structures (e.g., grammatical patterns, semantic elements, indexicals) predispose individuals to see the world in certain ways and influence the manner in which they act. The roots of this idea can be traced back to the Romanticism of the late eighteenth century and the notion that language reflects the spirit of the nation. During the first half of the twentieth century, linguistic anthropologists Franz Boas, Edward Sapir, and Benjamin Lee Whorf wrestled with questions of language diversity, linguistic codes, perception, and the ways language mediates between individuals and the larger world on a daily basis. In his highly influential article, "The Relation of Habitual Thought and Behavior to Language" (1941), Whorf, an insurance adjuster who turned to the study of linguistics, opens with a discussion of insurance claim cases where the origins of fires seem most clearly explained by people's linguistic understandings of the situations prior to the disasters they caused. In one case, a cigarette butt was thrown into what the person understood to be an "empty gasoline drum"; the container was, in fact, filled with explosive fumes. Later in the article Whorf goes on to consider the Hopi language and its grammatical system of classification, and compares this to "Standard Average European" (SAE), a lumping term he uses for Western European languages. Thus, for example, in Hopi plural forms are only used for actually existing material objects and not for abstractions such as "time." A Hopi speaker would not say "she stayed ten days" but rather something like "she left on the 11th day" or "she left after the 10th day." What SAE treats as a "length of time" is for Hopi a relation between two events, in this case the difference between a person's arrival and departure. Whorf explores additional differences in the "linguistic habits" and "the habitual thought worlds" of speakers of Hopi and SAE (and note here that Whorf is stressing the ruts of habit, not saying that people cannot see beyond their own language forms). Whorf's ideas, in turn, have inspired contemporary social scientists such as John Lucy to conduct field-based cognitive tests with speakers of Yucatec Maya and English, the results of which support the idea of a link between the structure of language and people's habitual practices.

Other participants in the linguistic relativity debate focus on the role of metaphors in shaping how people understand the world. When people speak metaphorically, they are using language to locate similarities *(continued)*

The Linguistic Relativity Hypothesis

(continued from page 105) in different cultural spheres and transfer meaning between these. Here, too, language may be seen as mediating between individuals and their routine experiences of the world. The work of George Lakoff and Mark Johnson (1980) in particular explores how central metaphors may condition the way people think and act. They propose, for example, that there is a widespread metaphorical paradigm in American English that equates "time" with "money": Time may be wasted, saved, spent, invested, budgeted, borrowed, and so on. Corresponding to the pervasiveness of this metaphor, speakers of American English act as if time is a valuable commodity—like money— and they understand the concept of time as a thing that can be spent, wasted, saved, or invested. Kaqchikel concepts, such as *k'u'x* or "heart" (discussed in Chapter 5), may also serve a similar axiomatic function for speakers of that language, providing metaphorical links to ideas of well-being, destiny, and sociabilty.

sulate a view of proper social relations between individuals of different generations, and they give a sense of the slightly uneven footing of the conversational terrain. They also show the interlocutor's adherence to a system of respect for traditional authority, which sets the basic cultural terms for engagement.

A shift away from the use of Mayan languages has also been of central concern to pan-Maya activists in Guatemala, including a number from Tecpán. Indeed, the present movement first publicly organized around several linguistic conferences held in the mid–1980s to promote a unified system of writing Mayan languages and thereby, it was hoped, to stimulate their use. In part this was political expediency, as language reform was seen as an effective—although not an overtly political—vehicle through which Maya groups could safely press for changes in government policy. But Maya activists also firmly believe that language is at the heart of Maya culture. Demetrio Cojtí Cuxil, a Tecpáneco who holds a Ph.D. from the University of Louvain in Belgium and also writes under his Mayan name Waqi' Q'anil, states that "Maya people exist because they have and speak their own languages" (1990: 12). This sentiment is expressed by Kaqchikel speakers from all walks of life—and not just activists—who, while aware of the linguistic prejudices of the larger society and pragmatic about the worth of mastering Spanish (and English), also see "their language" as a crucible of Maya culture. In fact, one could argue that underlying all these statements of the importance of Mayan languages to Maya cultural preservation is the tacit acceptance of a theoretical formulation known in anthropology as the linguistic relativity hypothesis, which asserts a link between language use and worldview (see box).

One of the means by which Kaqchikel Mayan has been given greater status and a more concrete role in the transmission of cultural information is via books and other publications written in or about the language. During the 1980s and 1990s there were an impressive number of efforts to put Kaqchikel in print, whether in the form of grammars and dictionaries, the recorded tales of elders, newspaper articles, legal documents, or school textbooks. Tecpanecos have played key roles in a number of these efforts. For example, Raxche' (Demetrio Rodríguez Guaján) has been central in the establishment and current operation of the Cholsamaj Press, which steadily issues works in Spanish by Maya writers on the Maya as well as books in Kaqchikel or Kaqchikel and Spanish. Examples in the bilingual category are *Kojtz'ib'an pa Kaqchi'/Leamos y escribamos Kaqchikel* (*Let's Read and Write Kaqchikel*) (1994), *Nuk'ulem chi rij kib'anikil chuqa' kich'ojib'al ri Achamaq'i'/Acuerdo sobre identidad y derechos de los Pueblos Indígenas* (*The Accord on the Identity and Rights of Indigenous People*) (1997), and *Runa'oj ri K'amöl B'ey Seattle/La carta del Jefe Seattle* (*Chief Seattle's Letter*) (1996). A number of Tecpanecos are also authors of books, including Demetrio Cojtí Cuxil and Raxche' (mentioned above), communication specialist Pedro Guoron Ajquijay, and linguist Pakal B'alam (José Obispo Rodríguez Guaján). It is notable that all of these writers have also been involved in educational efforts of some sort, whether in the schooling of children, adult education, educational policy, or the publication of academic texts.

Increasingly, schools have also become the site of Maya language and culture transmission. In a noteworthy change from years past, Kaqchikel is now found in some Tecpán schools, although for a variety of reasons and with a range of reactions from parents. For example, in 1998 there were three public schools in town that offered bilingual education for their youngest students. These and similar efforts in other Maya towns and villages aim to ease the transition into Spanish for Kaqchikel-speaking children and are supported by a relatively well-funded national government program of bilingual education. Many of the bilingual pedagogical materials used in the public schools have been produced with funding from the U.S. Agency for International Development (USAID), which has long supported bilingual education in Guatemala (see box). Students can also learn Kaqchikel if they are less than fluent speakers. Thus, for example, Tecpán's "middle school" (the public institution that teaches grades 7, 8, and 9) offers after-hours classes in Kaqchikel for Indian and *ladino* students.

Reactions to these different school language programs run the spectrum and show important points of debate. Some Maya parents are dissatisfied with the situation for the youngest students because, at best, the school programs only partly soften the rough transition to Spanish for the approximately 14 percent of the young school-aged population that speak little or no Spanish (these are 1994 figures). Others, speaking about Kaqchikel language classes, see these lessons as

USAID and Maya Education

Most humanitarian and development aid given by the U.S. government goes through USAID. In absolute terms the United States gives a great deal of aid around the world, some $8.8 billion in 1998. Throughout the Cold War years following World War II, the United States was by far the world's most generous nation (although arguably with its own self-interest at heart). But this role began to decline in the 1990s. By 1998, foreign aid accounted for only 0.3 percent of the U.S. budget, far less than most European countries in per capita terms and exceeded by Japan in absolute terms. One beneficiary of U.S. aid to Guatemala has been bilingual (Maya-Spanish) education, part of a broader U.S. goal to promote "inclusiveness" in the governments of troubled multicultural countries such as Guatemala. In this case the goal is to bring the Maya population—children and adults alike—into national life, make them participants in the political system that governs their country, and make government more representative. And it all starts with education, by training and thereby preparing Maya peoples to take on new roles. One element of this effort has been the publication of books. USAID funding and support, along with input from Guatemalan institutions, has led to the publication of bilingual dictionaries, primers, and guide books. An example is a guide—entitled *Una oportunidad para Marta Julia* in Spanish and *Ruq'ijul ruk'aslemal xta Marta Julia* in Kaqchikel (1998) and published jointly by USAID, the University of Rafael Landívar, and the Guatemalan Office for Human Rights—that discusses and promotes women's rights. It includes chapters on the importance of child welfare to women *and* men, the worth of women's work, self-confidence and self-awareness, public participation, and issues of equality.

diluting students' focus on improving their Spanish, the language of "the practical" (e.g., government and commerce). Some of these people assign Kaqchikel to the realm of the "cultural" and more suitable for home instruction. However, others point out that it *is* practical and necessary to speak Kaqchikel. As one Maya mother said to her son (who was moaning about having to do his Kaqchikel homework): "Say you're a doctor and you have a patient who says to you, '*Yalan niq'axon ri nuwi' y niq'axon nupam.*' ('My head hurts a lot and I have a stomach ache.') How are you going to understand her so you can treat her?" Some *ladinos* in town predictably oppose the presence of Kaqchikel of any sort in the curriculum because it debases their children's education. Yet other people, generally more ethnically aware Maya professionals, argue that the curriculum is not Maya enough, that current textbooks simply translate Spanish concepts rather than presenting (and legitimating) indigenous knowledge.

In 1993, in response to some of these concerns, a small group of local activists opened Iximche' Taluchi, a private nonprofit summer language and culture school with ties to the national Academy of Mayan Languages. The first offerings were classes on spoken and written Kaqchikel and K'iche' for Kaqchikel speakers. Somewhat ironically, enrolling in any of these entitled students to take a free class in either English or German, taught by Ted and his wife Mareike. Classes were first held in a borrowed room of the municipal hall, but soon moved to a rented house down the street. Iximche' Taluchi's initial success sparked an interest among the organizers to start a full-time private Maya school (*colegio*) for primary students. Through some amazing luck, the group came to the attention of a wealthy German philanthropist traveling in Guatemala and looking for projects to fund; he ended up offering to pay for the school's start-up costs, running expenses for five years, and construction of a new building (although the building has yet to be constructed). In 1996 the school—the Centro Educativo Ixmukane—opened in rented space, offering classes in first through third grades. Since then it has grown steadily, and by 2000 was teaching up through the sixth grade. The curriculum is a mix of standard primary school subjects with a substantial portion of Maya content. Students, for example, are exposed to Maya history from a Maya perspective, although it is perhaps a somewhat idealized historical perspective (but such is the norm in primary school texts everywhere). Even though the majority of lessons are taught in Spanish, students have classes on Kaqchikel language, using Kaqchikel not just as means to teach other things, but as a subject worthy of study in itself (as is Spanish). Parents send their children to this school for multiple reasons, some specifically for the Maya language and culture orientation of the curriculum, some in spite of that (more for reasons of cost or proximity to home), but none without some level of contemplation of the ethnicity issues raised by the existence of the institution.

What should emerge from this brief discussion of language as an identity marker is a sense of the relationships between ethnicity and linguistic issues. However, the construction of Maya identity in Tecpán becomes even more complex when we add indigenous clothing to the mix. Whereas Indian women are more likely than Indian men to be monolingual in a Mayan language, high percentages of both sexes speak a Mayan language in a community like Tecpán. With Maya clothing the situation is different: Women regularly wear *traje indígena* while men rarely do. And while the most elaborate ritual speech is generally the domain of men, Maya women unquestionably wear the most elaborate and densely meaningful articles of Indian dress. How then do Tecpanecos think about situations such as the indigenous fair-committee's presentation of young women wearing Maya clothing from throughout the highlands where a master of ceremonies—a local Indian man speaking eloquent Kaqchikel in support of Maya traditions—is dressed in blue jeans, a flannel shirt, and sunglasses?

THE FABRIC OF CULTURAL IDENTITY

There is scarcely a tourist, foreign-language student, or gringo anthropologist in Guatemala who doesn't arrive with the knowledge that much of *traje* is place-specific and that a person can often look at a handwoven blouse and immediately name the community from which it comes. This knowledge that *traje* pieces may be identified with towns comes to foreigners via guide books, *National Geographic*, museum exhibits, and TV travel shows. And it empowers visitors to read the human landscape with a certain insight even when they are newly arrived in the country and otherwise feeling lost.

The *traje*-town connection is a powerful and important element of cultural information—for foreigners and locals alike—because it so visibly links a person to a *pueblo* (in the sense both of a place and a people); however, it is only one of many relationships that enable Indians in Guatemala to signal different aspects of their identities via dress. Perhaps less obvious to the outside observer but nonetheless evident for local residents is the ability of *traje* to reflect, or at least suggest, information about wealth, gender, age, religion, worldliness, and beauty, as well as a wide range of issues having to do with ethnicity. What is more, the relationship of dress to place or religion or history is never a simple mechanical equation that can be learned like a list of foreign words and their meanings. Along with the nuanced and shifting identity relationships between *traje* and the people who wear it and/or see it being worn is an emotional content, a feeling toward *traje*, oneself in *traje*, or another person wearing *traje* that emerges in the day-to-day interactions of people for

Figure 6.2   Members of a weaving association wearing typical Tecpaneco styles.

Figure 6.3   Women wearing a Tecpán-style rij po't.

whom this clothing is supersaturated with meaning. Our aim in this section is to tease out some of the meanings, sentiments, and senses of ethnic identity that come from wearing (or not wearing) *traje* in Tecpán. These emerge as we discuss how *traje* has changed in recent years yet continues to remain "traditional," and how Tecpanecos construct and use *traje* to convey what it means to be an active, engaged Kaqchikel Maya in their community, country, and world today. (For more on *traje* in Tecpán, see Hendrickson 1995; see also Otzoy 1996.)

Clothing in the highlands is generally divided into *vestido* or *ropa corriente* ("dress" or "common clothes"), with its Western culture, and *tzyäq* or *traje* (also "dress"—in Kaqchikel and Spanish—but here with the sense of "Maya clothing"). The basic elements of a woman's *traje* are a *po't* or *huipil* (blouse), *uq* or *corte* (skirt), and *ximb'al* or *faja* (belt). In Tecpán, blouses consist of a rectangle of backstrap-woven cloth approximately thirty-six inches by forty-eight inches, folded in half and sewn so as to leave room for arm and head holes. Skirts are generally six yard lengths of cloth that has been woven on a treadle loom; this is sewn in a tube, then wrapped and folded around a woman's waist and secured with a handwoven belt that is also wrapped around the waist and the end tucked under (See Figure 6.2.). In addition to the "regular" *po't*, which is worn daily by women and tucked inside the *uq*, there is an "overblouse" (*rij po't* or *sobrehuipil*) that is worn over a "regular" *huipil* and used only by older women for special occasions. (See Figure 6.3.) The Tecpán *rij po't* has strong associations with both traditional Tecpán Maya culture *and* the Catholic Church. For example, women wear *rij po't* when they participate in activities of the *cofradías*, or religious brotherhoods, of the

Catholic Church or for certain ceremonies in Maya religion. Evangelical Maya would not participate in either of these and so normally do not own *rij po't*. However, Evangelical Maya recognize the intrinsic association of the *rij po't* with being Kaqchikel from Tecpán and in general don't have a problem, say, if a girl in their family needs to play the part of an older Maya woman in a school skit. This woman (or the girl who plays her) would be marked as older, revered, and knowledgeable about indigenous traditions by the *rij po't* she wears. And the family would need to borrow the piece or might have one in their possession as an heirloom from, say, a deceased relative who was Catholic.

Although there are town-specific versions of each of these *traje* pieces, Kaqchikel women generally wear generic forms of skirts and belts that signal that the wearer is Maya but don't give place-specific information of particular cultural importance. The opposite is generally true with the *po't* (or *rupam po't*, "inside *po't*" because it is tucked into a skirt). There are a number of styles of *po't* that are specific to Tecpán, and some Tecpanecas wear versions of these all the time. These women are often weavers who also speak of the tremendous pride they have in working on their backstrap looms and creating beautiful pieces; all of this maps into a strong allegiance to the community. Others, however, wear Tecpán *po't* only occasionally; for example, when they specifically want to signal their town membership or because they just happen to feel like it that particular day. Reasons for this differential use of town *traje* vary and are socially significant. Tecpán *huipiles* are very expensive, and a woman must either be able to weave her

Figure 6.4   Woman weaving a po't on a backstrap loom.

Figure 6.5   Traje vendor at the Thursday market in Tecpán.

own blouses using a backstrap loom (see Figure 6.4) or else have enough money to buy them, for example at the market, at prices ranging from approximately $25 to $75 (this being the equivalent of one-sixth to one-half of a grade school teacher's monthly salary).

Because of economic issues, the majority of women at least occasionally wear cheaper treadle loom blouses from Totonicapán or Quetzaltenango or ones machine-embroidered on machine-made cloth. Some very poor women might also opt to wear T-shirts or second-hand blouses, which are even cheaper. Women from other towns who marry into Tecpán families may retain the use of *traje* from their natal communities even as they dress their daughters in the *traje* from their new homes (or the mothers and daughters might wear *huipiles* from both communities). In addition, in recent years there has been a growing pan-Maya sentiment that motivates the use of *traje* from other communities. Women—especially more traveled and professional women with contacts well beyond Tecpán—wear different *traje* pieces because they admire the beauty of the different color schemes and design motifs, can demonstrate their ability to procure items that are hard to find locally, and signal their identity as Maya (in the sense of *all* Maya) rather than as an *indígena* from Tecpán (or any other community). The use of a variety of *traje*, then,

Figure 6.6   Tecpán's
indigenous queen, 1980.

can be seen as a statement about ethnic identity where the group affiliation marked
is "Guatemalan Maya" rather than "Kaqchikel Maya from Tecpán."

But how does any of this play out in real life circumstances in Tecpán? A couple of cases can serve as illustrations. Each year for the municipal fair honoring
the patron saint of Tecpán—Saint Frances of Assisi—at least four young women
are selected as queens. *Ladinas* fill the positions of Queen of the Franciscan
Fiestas and Godmother of Sports, while Kaqchikeles are selected Queen Iximché
(referring to the precontact Kaqchikel capital) and Queen Ixmucané (the creator
ancestor who ground the corn from which the first humans were made). Without
exception the indigenous candidates wear Tecpán *huipiles* for the competition,
and some even wear *rij po't* and old-style, Tecpán-specific skirts—called
morgas—to signal their awareness of and adherence to Tecpán's *costumbres*. (See
Figure 6.6.) After the indigenous queens are selected, they continue to wear
Tecpán *traje* for all official duties, especially if they are invited to attend a queen's
competition in a neighboring municipality. There the young women's clothing is
important because it not only reflects a pride in being Indian but also tells the audience what town they are from. What is more, the young woman who holds the
crown of Queen Ixmucané marks her position by wearing a cape fashioned from
the fabric of the *rij po't*. Here the handwoven cloth links the piece to the Maya ancestors while the shape signals its association to the young queen.

But not all *traje* worn by Tecpanecas is from Tecpán. For example, when Carol visits Guatemala she stays with her friend Claudia, whom she first met in 1980. At that point Claudia was just starting a career as a teacher and social worker and, during those first years on the job, was able to purchase a number of *traje* pieces from different highland communities, sometimes going through school friends or purchasing them on travels of her own. She admired the *traje* from other communities and wore these pieces with pride to show the women she worked with that a Maya—so identified by her dress—could hold a government job with considerable responsibility. One of the outfits she bought in those early years was a *huipil* and *corte* from Chichicastenango, a town renowned for its beautiful weaving (and often referred to as Chichi). In 1999 Carol spent several months in Guatemala, living with Claudia and her family. By that point the Chichi skirt was quite faded and old, although the blouse seemed as good as new. Carol had mentioned wanting to go to the Chichicastengo market to look at *huipiles* before she left Guatemala and so, for her going-away "party," Claudia and her husband organized a shopping expedition to Chichi's big Sunday market. There Carol located a blouse she liked—one with traditional Chichi design motifs of the two-headed eagle—and Claudia found a *corte* with elaborate tie-dyed designs and embroidery. Because she also likes dressing her two daughters in *traje* from other towns (but couldn't afford much more right then), she settled on Chichi belts for the girls, ones that she knew were unavailable in the Tecpán market.

Whereas virtually all Tecpán women who consider themselves *indígenas* wear *traje*, that is not the case with men. In some communities, men of all ages wear indigenous clothing that is distinctive to the municipality. In Tecpán, however, men's everyday *traje* is actually more of a regional style that can be seen in Comalapa, Santa Apolonia, and other neighboring towns. It is composed of white pants, a blue or white shirt, dark wool jacket, hat, sandals, and a *rodillera* (a rectangle of black-and-white-checked wool cloth with fringe on two ends) that is folded in half and secured at the waist by a multicolored handwoven belt. Men's use of this *traje* is more or less disappearing with the oldest generation; virtually no men under the age of seventy wear *traje* on a daily basis, and this includes Tecpán men involved in the Maya revitalization movement (See Figure 6.7). Although these individuals might promote the preservation of *costumbre* (indigenous customs), work to improve their own command of Kaqchikel Mayan, and encourage women to preserve the use of *tzyäq*, the closest many come to using traditional *traje* is to wear a style of sandal that is recognized as "Indian" and perhaps white jeans, which have the "look" of the locally produced white pants. We should add that there are a couple of forms of Maya men's ritual wear and these are seen more today than twenty years ago. For example, the dark blue woolen poncho used by male members of *cofradías* is being revived after falling out of use for decades. And *aj q'ija'*, Maya spiritual leaders, who are growing in number and seen more publicly, also wear ritual *traje*, including handwoven belts and headcloths as well as white pants. On a related but somewhat different note,

Figure 6.7   Family with males in traje and in Western dress.

in the late 1980s and early 1990s a style of bomber jacket was designed that had elements of backstrap-woven designs from Tecpán attached to either side of the zipper and additional designs on the chest and sleeves. This jacket became something of an emblem of "membership" in the pan-Maya movement, although subsequent years have seen both a proliferation of styles used by indigenous males as well as the original jacket now on sale for tourists (See Figure 6.8).

These culturally motivated men, who wear *traje* infrequently if at all, are not unaware of the irony in the contrast between "what they say" and "what they do." How can they exhibit such immense pride in all things Maya and yet not dress in *traje*? How can they praise and identify with women's *traje* and yet not wear the men's? Various men explain their actions by pointing to the prejudices held by *ladinos* against Indians, the virtual impossibility of hiding one's ethnic identity when wearing *traje*, and men's greater participation in the often non-Maya world beyond home, market stalls, and *milpa* fields in Tecpán. A man in *traje* would be too prejudiced against, they say: better to wear *vestido*. If asked "But what about women? They wear *traje!*" common responses include mentioning that women are less likely to deal with national agents (government loan officers, military recruiters, etc.), that women's *traje* is exceedingly beautiful and more appreciated in the larger world, and that the men simply weren't raised in *traje* and can't make the change in mid-life. Once, however, when Carol asked that question, her male respondent answered that women "*son más valientes.*" ("are braver [than men]"). Whether it is a matter of bravery or the sheer necessity of facing a prejudiced

Figure 6.8
Pakal B'alam wearing
a jacket made using
traditional textile patterns.

world in clothing that they do not want to give up, Tecpán women much more than men perpetuate clothing traditions on a daily basis as mothers, vendors, weavers, school teachers, bank tellers, and social workers in their home community and beyond.

If adults find themselves fully socialized into particular ways of dressing—with clothing habits (like linguistic habits) that are hard to break under routine circumstances—what about children? A baby, for example, doesn't have particular expectations regarding the clothes it will wear. However, parents and relatives and neighbors of the parents certainly do, and the parents dress their children accordingly. Children nonetheless don't end up as exact miniatures of their parents. There are clothing norms for children that differ from those of adults. Also, adults have their own theories about what they want their children to wear, how they want them to be seen in public, and what they want their children to be able to do (which different clothes might help or hinder). And soon enough children develop their own ideas about what they want on their bodies. Thus, for example, over the last twenty years there has been a notable increase in Kaqchikel girls' use of Western dress, which has tremendous status through its links to global media and lifestyles seen on television and video. Whereas their mothers might have worn *traje* every waking moment of their lives from age one or two on (including when they played basketball or soccer at school), their daughters now wear gym clothes for recreation and might lounge around the house or do household chores on weekends wearing sweatpants, T-shirts, and sneakers. Many parents see clear distinctions between this public, recreational use and private, "grubby," or leisure-time, home use of *vestido*, on the one hand, versus the use of *traje* for more formal or proper public and private occasions when the woven emblems of ethnicity are a must. That doesn't mean the children always agree. "But why do I have to wear my *corte*?" a child complains as she pulls at the waist of her skirt and contorts her face as if she were in pain. Her mother responds with the equivalent of "Because . . ." to the child, while telling the anthropologist that the child's problem with *traje* is that she wore *vestido* so often when she was very small that she's just not used to having the *corte* and *faja* wrapped tightly around her waist: A body needs to get used to the constraints put on it by particular articles of dress, and the little girl simply isn't used to *traje* yet. Boys are socialized into the sorts of clothes they will wear their entire lives: Jeans, T-shirts, sweatshirts, and Nikes are favorites for leisure use, and button-down shirts and formal pants are part of school uniforms.

Another *traje*-related change that has affected girls more than boys is the decline in children learning to weave on the backstrap loom, an activity that is seen as linking Kaqchikel women to their pre-Conquest ancestors and that is seen as symbolic of Maya women's work in the household. This shift in who is weaving is particularly notable for girls whose families live in the center of town and who have easy access to schools, at least through the ninth grade. This was not always the case for their mothers and grandmothers, as the educational opportunities in the municipality were significantly fewer even one generation ago, and families more often chose not to educate daughters (and sons sometimes) beyond primary school because they thought that education was not what girls needed for life. According to this line of thought, being able to weave on a backstrap loom assured for a woman the ability to make clothes for herself and her daughters as well as the possibility of making some money by weaving for sale outside the home. Girls who went on in school found themselves having to choose between homework and learning to weave; both took a lot of time and occurred at basically the same time in life. (Girls typically start to weave between the ages of seven and ten.) And while weaving is a flexible job for women who want or need to balance childrearing, cleaning, gardening, and cooking at home with hours at the loom, it pays very little (often as low as 25 to 50 cents per day) compared to even the most modest salaried jobs in town. This is not to say that backstrap weaving is disappearing in Tecpán, as it is in other communities (see Ehlers 1990). There are still a large number of weavers in the town center and, even more, in the rural areas. However, it is somewhat ironic that the people who wear the most extraordinarily elaborate and beautiful *huipiles* are either weavers, who weave for themselves (or their daughters), or women with professional jobs, who generally don't weave at all but who can afford the most expensive pieces.

Another irony is that weaving, such a "traditional" art, is also one of the principal means by which clothing in Tecpán and surrounding communities has changed in recent years. Much of this change is embraced and the results celebrated as *el mero traje* of Tecpán (with *mero* used here to give the sense of "real" or "authentic"). However, not every innovation receives this label, which raises the question: How can *traje* change and still remain "the same," "traditional," and a direct descendant of the dress of the Kaqchikel ancestors? The answer is not easy or predictable, but creations over the past twenty years have played with innovative color combinations (with the traditional design motifs remaining intact); the scale, complexity, and spacing of figures; and the introduction of different sorts of realistic floral and fruit designs in combination with the older geometric figures. Agreement about these innovations is never uniform, however, and the logic weavers use both for innovating on the loom as well as explaining why they think particular pieces qualify as "Tecpán *traje*" provides rich cultural data on the material expression of ethnic identity.

KAQCHIKEL MAYAN AND *TRAJE*: RESONATING ISSUES

The Accord on the Identity and Rights of Indigenous Peoples, signed 31 March 1995, was one element of a longer peace process that brought a formal end to Guatemala's thirty-five-year civil war. In detailed terms both the government of Guatemala and the organization of guerrilla groups (the Unidad Revolucionaria Nacional Guatemalteca, or URNG) agreed on a number of cultural rights, including ones having to do with Mayan languages and *traje*. Very early in the document a section on language states: "Language is one of the pillars that supports culture, being in particular the vehicle for the acquisition and transmission of the indigenous cosmovision, of its cultural knowledge and values. In this sense, all the languages spoken in Guatemala deserve equal respect" (Saq'be Editorial 1997: 24–27, our translation). This is followed shortly thereafter by a section on *traje* that proclaims: "The constitutional right to wear *traje* ought to be respected and guaranteed in all circles of national life" (1997: 34–35). Then there is mention of a conscience-raising campaign needed to inform Guatemalans of "the spiritual and cultural value of indigenous clothing and the respect it is owed" (1997: 34–35), where "indigenous" is specifically said to refer to the Maya, Garifuna, and Xinca (the latter two being small groups of approximately 6,500 and 300 living in the eastern part of the country).

In Tecpán there was no immediate and massive impact from the agreement on these and other rights. For certain issues, the Accord was a culminating gesture for ongoing progress made during the previous several years. Thus, people gradually (and to varying degrees) have become aware of the document and its guarantees. Tecpanecos read articles in the national press in which indigenous families protest school rules that force all students to wear school uniforms; now they have the guarantee that their children can wear *traje* to school if they so desire. Parents also cannot be forced by municipal authorities to give Christian names for official birth certificates, and so more children with Maya names like Pakal, Nikte, and Tojil have began to appear in town records. And government social workers, in some cases bearing newly printed literature in Kaqchikel and Spanish, work to educate people on these issues. People's sense is that Guatemala still has a long way to go to achieve ethnic equality, but the events of the 1990s were propitious.

Tecpanecos have taken active roles in other government initiatives that likewise have had impacts on issues concerning Kaqchikel Mayan and *traje*, their prominence and people's sense of cultural worth. Within the Academy of Mayan Languages of Guatemala, Tecpanecos have participated in the creation of a unified alphabet for all *idiomas mayas*. Whereas before a number of different alphabets were in use, even for the same language—something that made reading a confusing endeavor—with the congressionally approved unified alphabet, Mayan texts have begun moving toward uniformity. This is the alphabet now in use for Kaqchikel language readers in Tecpán's schools.

The Guatemalan government and several NGOs have also taken a role in promoting the diversification of handwoven objects, with an eye toward new or increased sales of "handicrafts" to foreign markets. (Some see this term as demeaning: why not "arts?" [Sam Colop 1996: 113, citing Eduardo Galeano].) Different weavers' cooperatives in Tecpán are hopeful that these opportunities will help them reap economic benefits while allowing them to continue their traditional art. However, pitfalls to their success include the lack of contacts abroad (or the need for outsider intermediaries), the amount of work needed to make a piece versus the price it can bring (this, in part, is due to foreigners' ignorance of the time involved in backstrap weaving), and a lack of local knowledge of the needs and desires of foreign buyers. Examples on this last count include preferences for different color palettes in Tecpán versus New York or Tokyo and different consumer needs mapping into objects that are common to foreign buyers but virtually unknown to weavers (e.g., fanny packs, eyeglass cases, friendship bracelets, and covers for big fluffy couch pillows are not items normally used in Tecpán, although these sell well to tourists).

Tecpanecos involved in traditional arts have, in the past, received government money to advertise the town and buying opportunities for visitors. In the early 1990s a color brochure was produced by INGUAT (the Guatemalan Tourist Institute) with local input. It featured Tecpán as an important Indian market destination with textiles as a principal item for purchase. This was a case of Maya using the ethnic emblem of *traje* (as well as locally made rugs, wood carvings, and more) to woo potential buyers. When publications are conceived solely by INGUAT, Tecpanecos can be much more critical of the government's use of images of Indians as a lure for tourists. "Guatemala: Colorful and Friendly" (an oft-used slogan from the early 1990s when the civil war was still very much a fact of everyday life) is repeatedly represented by Indians dressed in brilliant *traje*, whose exoticness is enhanced by narratives such as: "The arrival of the Spanish brought new ways to Guatemala. Mixed and merged with those of the Indian descendants of the Maya and verbally handed down from father to son over generations, they have formed the idiosyncrasies which are such a charming facet of today's Guatemala" (Instituto Guatemalteco de Turismo 1992: 3). Aside from questions about contemporary Indians being "descendants of the Maya" (and not Maya themselves?) and the use of terms such as "idiosyncrasies" and "charming," there are larger questions such as: What is the impact of images like these on the people presented? Who reaps the major benefits from the visitors who are enticed by visions of "real Maya" (or, at least, "real Indians"), colorful *traje*, and the sound of exotic tongues?

This takes us back to some of the issues we introduced at the start of this chapter. Ethnic markers that "work" must be easily identifiable, regularly employed, and important to the people involved. This does not mean, however, that different groups of people won't regularly assign different meanings and uses to what is important to them. Language and *traje* can have profound and complex but different meanings for different people or for the same people but at different times. The importance of both Kaqchikel Mayan and Tecpán *traje* lies both with the number of cultural issues that can be understood through them as well as their ability to change—and hence remain meaningful—over time.

Further Reading

Garzon, Susan, R. McKenna Brown, Julia Becker Richards, and Wuqu' Ajpub' (Arnulfo Simón). 1998. *The life of our language: Kaqchikel Maya maintenance, shift, and revitalization.* Austin: University of Texas Press.

Hendrickson, Carol. 1991. Images of the Indian in Guatemala: The role of indigenous dress in Indian and Ladino constructions. In *Nation-states and Indians in Latin America,* edited by Greg Urban and Joel Sherzer, pp. 287–306. Austin: University of Texas Press.

Oxlajuuj Keej Maya' Ajtz'iib' 1993. *Maya' chii': Los idiomas mayas de Guatemala.* Guatemala City: Editorial Cholsamaj.

Tecpán's central plaza on Wednesday afternoon and Thursday morning (1994).

7

The Land and Its Fruits: Cultural Associations in Changing Economic Times

Tecpán undergoes a dramatic transformation starting each Wednesday afternoon as the large regional market grows to fill the center of town. By early Thursday morning the open expanses of Tecpán's central plaza and park and all the streets leading to them are covered in market stalls, the most elaborate found in front of the municipal building and extending over toward the Catholic church. Several yards wide and a yard or two deep, these mega-stalls are constructed of poles lashed together by rope and covered with plastic tarps. The largest are places where men and women sell a variety of *traje*-related items: Maya skirt material, handwoven blouses, shawls, belts, and carrying clothes. In other areas, medium to small-sized versions of the same shelter a wide variety of merchandise—pots and pans, spices, ropes, alarm clocks and flashlights, dried fish, bread, fruits, and vegetables—while closer to the outer edges of the market vendors may simply spread a tarp or cloth on the ground and lay out their knitted sweaters, used clothing, farm tools, loom sticks, ceramic pots, pineapples, or recycled flour sacks.

It is a massive mobilization, all the more incredible for its weekly regularity. The municipal government collects a modest fee from each vendor (a few quetzals at most, depending on the size of the stall), and an army of buses brings vendors and buyers from outlying *aldeas* and towns throughout the region. The market is remarkably well-organized, although it gives the visitor the impression of barely controlled chaos. Many North Americans are uncomfortable shopping in the midst of crushing crowds and haggling over prices. Locals, while used to the bargaining and aware of the exact location of a favorite vendor for tomatoes or thread, sometimes also complain about the crush of people and goods, the difficulty of walking down narrow aisles while lugging baskets of purchases, and the occasional presence of pickpockets. Still, the prices are generally reasonable, the variety abundant, and many things are available in town only at the Thursday market.

When economists speak of markets, they are rarely referring to the sort of concrete places and myriad individual monetary exchanges occupying the center of Tecpán every Thursday. In their usage, markets are much broader, even abstract, entities; they are talked about as places, but they are virtual places. Thus we speak of the global oil market or the national market for pork bellies or simply "the market." Commentators often endow such abstract markets with human-like agency: "the market says we are in for a downturn," "the market is bullish," and so on. Of course, markets themselves are simply aggregate representations of individual human actions taking place in numerous sites, but in press reports and everyday conversation they take on a life of their own. Market forces, market desires, market fears—very often these are seen to control human action rather than vice versa.

In light of these larger senses of the term it is easy to see the Maya of Tecpán as long-suffering victims of the world market, from the injustices of the Conquest and colonial rule, to the institutionalization of discrimination in various forms, to the enduring inequality of landownership, to the violence of the 1980s, and to the current vagaries of the world market. But labeling the Maya as victims runs the risk of seeing them as mere reactants to outside forces rather than as intentional agents with a hand in the creation of their own lives and culture. In the Kaqchikel region, global market forces *have* changed how people live their lives, imposing new restrictions but also presenting new opportunities. Some people have prospered in these new economic relationships while others have suffered, although it is still too early to tell whether the economic benefits will outweigh the social costs for particular families or the community as a whole (or even how to make that assessment). Nonetheless, whether from necessity or desire, many Tecpán Maya actively pursue new forms of production in their attempts to maintain control over their means of economic production and their lives.

MILPA AGRICULTURE

Traditional Kaqchikel economic models are based on subsistence agriculture, with Maya men typically related to the land they work and Maya women to the products of the land, which they prepare for their families' use. In 1994 about half of the male heads-of-households in Tecpán's urban area were primarily farmers, and a high percentage of the other half worked part-time in agricultural pursuits. In Tecpán's *aldeas* the figure for farmers was even higher: 78 percent of male heads-of-household were full-time agriculturalists. Figures such as these are static, however, and don't give a sense of the trends over time or the dynamics within a given household as families work to cultivate their land as well as plan what education their children

Figure 7.1   Milpa *plot. Note the vines of beans growing up the corn stalk.*

will receive and hence what kind of work they will do in life. They also do not reflect the agricultural contributions of women. It is quite common today, for example, to find a grandfather of a family who has been a farmer his whole life, his wife having helped with plantings and harvests as well as tending the family's fruit tress. Their sons or sons-in-law might farm family plots on weekends while holding salaried jobs during the week (and hiring *mozos*, or day laborers, to supply additional labor). And the grandsons of the family, full-time students in local schools, might be encouraged to accompany their father to the family plot to learn to be *hombres de maiz* ("men of corn," as one family characterized the process, while also referring to Miguel Angel Asturias's book), something that may or may not appeal to ten- or twelve-year-olds who would also like to spend their Saturdays and Sundays hanging out with friends. Contemporary shifts in education and employment aside, the statistics show a persistence of farming as a way of life and lend credence to the claim that, for most Maya in Tecpán today, cultural wealth (if not always economic wealth) is seen ultimately to derive from the land (see Gudeman and Rivera 1990).

Maize (*Zea mays*) is the primary subsistence staple for most families in Tecpán, for Maya and *ladino* alike. Maize is characteristically grown in *milpas*, small plots of maize and beans interspersed with squashes, gourds, and sometimes coffee, tobacco, or fruit trees. *Milpa* agriculture has been practiced in the Maya region for millennia, and for good reason. Maize and bush dry beans (of the genus *Phaseolus*) are almost perfectly suited to be grown together. Maize is an especially nitrogen-hungry plant, and planted by itself it rapidly depletes the soil's natural fertility. But beans are nitrogen-rich plants, and when placed next to maize they are able to keep the soil's nitrogen levels in line. What is more, for a

Figure 7.2   Milpa *plots interspersed with other crops outside Tecpán.*

maximum harvest bush beans need to grow up (rather than on the ground), and the maize stalks provide a natural stake.

Maize and beans are the two anchors of the Maya diet, and a humble meal consists of no more than corn tortillas and beans. What is more, these two staples are not only agriculturally symbiotic but nutritionally complementary. Although maize and beans individually contain all the essential amino acids needed for the human diet, a person would need to eat large amounts of either one to fulfill minimal protein requirements on any given day. Eating the two together achieves something known as protein complementarity (where the complemented whole of the combined proteins is greater than the sum of the individual parts) and is an efficient way to supply growing children and working adults with the protein they need.

Tecpán's *milpa* agricultural cycle begins at the end of the dry season—usually in late April but sometimes as late as early June—with the burning of the old crop and the planting of the new. After six months of virtually no rain the brown dry stalks and vines catch fire easily, and in the weeks before the first rains the hills and plains around Tecpán are dotted with the wispy gray smoke of burning *milpas*. The ashes of last year's crop are then worked into the soil with large-bladed hand hoes; farmers often describe this as "feeding of the land," supplying the necessary nourishment to the land so that the land, in turn, will meet the farmers' needs. Maize kernels, selected from the best of last year's crop, are dropped three or so at a time into small holes, and a mixture of dirt and fertilizer is mounded on top of the seeds.

For many Tecpanecos, the moon plays an important role in determining when they will plant their fields. Planting of traditional strains of maize has to take place at the beginning of the rainy season. If one plants too early, the seeds will wilt away for lack of water, and if one plants too late (once heavy rains have begun), the seeds may be washed away in a downpour. This fundamental limitation, which is made more challenging when dealing with the unpredictability of actual weather patterns, allows significant leeway in deciding the exact date of planting. Most Tecpaneco farmers try to schedule their *milpa* plantings on the day of a full moon, preferably the last full moon before rain is calculated to begin. They explain that a full moon exerts a pull on the seed that helps it grow and break out of the ground, not unlike the lunar influence on female fecundity.

After planting, farmers return frequently to their fields to check on the progress of their crops and make sure that nothing has disturbed them. There are three major periods of labor during the growing season, called the First Work, the Second Work, and the Third Work. The first takes place in early June, when the corn is about an inch or so high: Fields are weeded, fertilizer is applied, and soil is mounded around the tender stalks to protect them from Tecpán's sometimes vicious winds. This work is repeated in mid-August and again in mid-September for an optimal harvest, although economic hardships sometimes force families to forgo one or more of these labors. In addition, farmers short on ready cash may skip one or more applications of expensive chemical fertilizer, but this comes at the expense of harvest bounty. A few farmers still prefer manure supplied by cattle and pigs, but most use imported chemical fertilizers. Farmers, even as they themselves adopt the chemical fertilizers, see the switch as a mixed blessing at best, forcing them into a costly fertilizer regime that is not easily abandoned.

Fresh ears of local maize (*elotes*) begin appearing in the market in October (and earlier in warmer parts of Guatemala), but most are left attached to the stalk, which is doubled over, to dry for a couple of months after the rains have stopped. It is traditional for a family to harvest its maize crop before Christmas, but for various reasons a good part of the harvest continues into January. The dried ears are pulled from the stalk and bundled up in large nets to be carried home (in a pickup truck, preferably, or by horse or on one's back, if not). Back home, the *troje* (corn crib) has been cleaned out and readied for the new year's supply. At this point, a few families conduct formal Maya ceremonies to give thanks to the gods for the year's harvest and to ask for mercy with next year's crops. In its most elaborate form, the *entrojada* ("encribbing") ceremony lasts for three days and entails the considerable expenses of hiring musicians and feeding guests. Shorter and less elaborate celebrations include a special meal for the extended family and a few guests. For these occasions, the maize is separated by color and stored in segregated areas of the *troje*, as it is often intended for different uses: yellow maize to be eaten at deaths and births as well as at daily meals; white maize for fiestas; and blue-black (literally green—*räx*—in Kaqchikel) to provide variety in the daily diet. Red corn is rarely grown in Tecpán.

Economies and Cultures

Anthropologist Marshall Sahlins created a stir in 1972 with the publication of *Stone Age Economics*. The most widely cited chapter is titled "The Original Affluent Society," in which he argues that economics and anthropology have been unjust to hunter-gatherer societies, viewed through the eyes of Western observers raised in a market economy. Scarcity, he argues, is a myth of "civilization." People can be affluent by either wanting little or producing much. Among "primitive" peoples, economy is art, not science, and is fully integrated into culture; it is mistaken to believe that their wants are great and their means are limited. Wanting very little, then, people in "primitive" societies actually enjoy a very affluent society, with much leisure time to cultivate social pursuits (what Sahlins calls the "Zen road to affluence"). As societies move from hunting/gathering to agriculture to industrial modes of production, the amount of work per capita increases and the amount of leisure decreases. In other chapters Sahlins resurrects the largely forgotten work of Russian ethnologist A. V. Chayanov on peasant differentiation. Studying Russian peasant households in the late nineteenth and early twentieth centuries, Chayanov (1966 [1925]) found that in peasant households changes in farm size and productivity mirror the family demographic cycle. As more children are born there is a greater demand for food and so more is produced; as children grow older and establish their own households, families often divest part of their land holdings, either through inheritance or sales. In other words, Chayanov argued that Russian peasants produced just enough to get by; there was perhaps a small surplus, but not an evolution of farms growing ever larger in size (as Lenin, for example, argued—which is one reason Chayanov's work was so long forgotten). They value other things more than blind economic advancement, and would generally rather enjoy their leisure time than make more money. Tecpanecos, as a whole, are not ideologically opposed to capitalist enrichment, but there is an economy that also values the freedom and flexibility that goes with controlling one's means of production.

It is taboo (*xajan*) to intentionally waste maize, and at the harvest great care is taken to gather every bit. Often harvesting techniques follow a logic not bound by strict economic rationality, motivated by what economists call "distorting market factors" such as affective ties to the land and its produce. As an example, take the case of Estuardo, a Tecpaneco who lives with his family in the capital, where he and his wife have professional jobs. Nonetheless, he maintains his portion of the family lands, hiring a farmer with an adjoining plot to work the land in exchange for half of the harvest (a common arrangement called *mitad*). One February weekend in 1994, while Estuardo and his family were visiting in Tecpán, they took a day to go to the fields. The *mozo* and his helpers had already harvested the maize and beans, giving Estuardo his half, which would supply his family's needs for most of the coming year. Yet Estuardo and his family made the grueling drive and hike out to the fields, spending a full day gathering the leftover maize, ears missed on the stalk as well as ones dropped in the underbrush. It was a festive occasion, with the children having great fun, and his wife cooking a special meal of Tecpán's famous local sausages. The fields, which were meticulously neat just months before, were covered in broken stalks and dried vines. Two large nets (which might hold eight or ten basketballs) were filled with the last of the maize, and the family struggled to haul them back to the dirt trail and the car. The value of the maize collected was not much more than the cost of the food and gas expended, and certainly not an efficient use of the time of these two urban professionals. At stake was not the maize's 30 or 40 quetzals of market value, but rather its symbolic value as a sacred and life-giving product. No matter how well off one is, Eduardo explained, maize is not to be wasted.

This raises the question, then, of why the *mozo* would allow some of the precious corn to be left behind. Perhaps he was rushed at harvest time and needed to get back to his own fields, perhaps corn does not hold the same symbolic value for him, perhaps it was the work of his teenage sons who were less than thrilled about having to do the harvest—we should not allow a discussion of the spiritual values of corn to overshadow the imperatives of mundane practice. Undoubtedly, it is much different for urban professionals who romanticize their ties to the land from the comfort of their cosmopolitan lives than it is for a rural farmer bound to the tedious and strenuous quotidian labors of manual farming. But also, perhaps, the *mozo's* reasons were tied to the fact that this was not his land, it had not been passed down for generations through his family, and so its produce was less symbolically laden for him than for the owners of the land.

With the application of fertilizer, one *cuerda*[1] of *milpa* land in the Tecpán area produces on average of just over 6.3 *quintales* (a 100-pound measure) of maize per yearly harvest. An average Tecpán family (with 6.3 members) consumes over 3,000 pounds of maize annually, needing 4.8 *cuerdas* of land for their maize needs alone. Tecpaneco farmers would revise this estimate upward significantly, and most assume about 9 *cuerdas* to be the minimum necessary to support a family that wanted or needed to raise all its own corn. Almost 40 percent of Tecpanecos households own 9 *cuerdas* or less of land, reflecting in some cases a general poverty of resources and in others the maximum a family might be able to cultivate (or have cultivated for them by paid help) while also holding salaried jobs.

THE DANGEROUS AND BUCOLIC:
LANDS BEYOND THE EDGE OF TOWN

Just as maize is treated with a blend of cultural respect and market savvy, so too is the land on which it is grown. In speaking of land, Kaqchikel Tecpanecos often invest it with agency in phrases such as "the land gives us" or "the land no longer gives as it once did." It is not surprising that farmers have strong sentiments toward their land, their means of production. And such sentiments significantly affect how Tecpanecos choose to use their land and to make a living.

With few exceptions, *milpa* plots and other farmland in Tecpán are located outside of the fairly densely populated town center. (See Figure 7.3.) The most valuable of these lands lie on a fertile plain that skirts the southwest border of town; the least desirable are in the mountains to the northeast, up to several hours away on foot or bike (although much closer time-wise if one is so lucky as to own a motorcycle or truck). Owing to inheritance patterns as well as the buying and selling of land, households frequently own two or more non-contiguous *milpa* plots, often some distance apart, effectively thwarting efficiencies of scale. According to one understanding of the local ethno-geography, *milpa* plots and other farmlands occupy an intermediate area between the familiar and orderly structure of town and the unpredictable and potentially dangerous wilds. Tecpanecos make a clear distinction between the town and countryside, and city residents pride themselves on their urbanity. But while the *cabecera* serves as a symbolic archetype of ordered civilization, the wilds are seen as home to chaos and savagery (a metaphor used to deadly effect by the army in the early 1980s; see Richards 1985). Farmland is captured from the wild fecundity of nature, but it is only incompletely colonized by culture. These lands, especially distant plots, are seen to occupy a rich but potentially dangerous liminal space. Odd things often happen on the way to the *milpa* as one walks through the *monte*. It is here that *la llorona, duendes* (figures known to many other Latin American people than just the Maya), and other specters in the guise of beautiful maidens, dwarves, or animals sometimes appear, attempting to seduce passing farmers with sexual favors or riches and steal their souls.

Rural areas are also sites where antisocial human activities can take place and attempts be made to keep these hidden from the general public. In Tecpán the violence of the late 1970s and early 1980s first emerged on the outskirts of town, in small villages and hamlets as well as in other municipalities just beyond the town's borders, then crept into the municipal center itself. For example, in late 1980 one indication that violence was circling Tecpán was the movement of military vehicles under cover of darkness. At that time Carol was living in the *cabecera*, on a road that led out of town to the south and west. She and her neighbors would hear these vehicles passing along the roads at night, moving through the town and out into the forested mountains several kilometers distant. Occasionally there were explosive sounds like gunfire in the night. Occasionally,

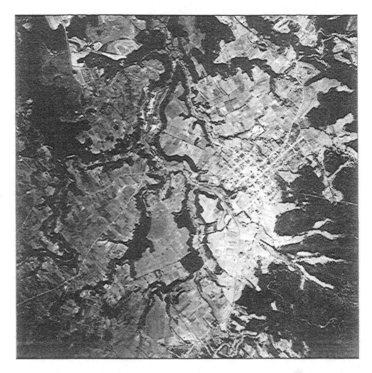

Figure 7.3
Tecpán's town
center and sur-
rounding fields
(1982).

too, reports would make it through the local grapevine of local military operations or deaths or other forms of destruction in these spaces outside of town but
in the vicinity of people's *milpas* or *aldeas* where relatives lived. The newspapers,
radios, and other "official" sources said virtually nothing about these activities, so
people were left to gather information and speculate on very individual bases.

Approximately a year before this stepped-up military presence, local activist
Chico Sisamit went public, protesting the abuses of Tecpán's municipal forests,
which are supposed to be accessible to members of the community who have permission for very specific projects (e.g., what we might call the sustainable harvesting of firewood). By this time the forests had been heavily lumbered—the hillsides
raped, some said—and fingers pointed to local officials who were judged to have
abused their municipal powers to gain substantial personal wealth from the sale of
the wood and to have hidden their actions by operating in this less-inhabited area.
Chico Sisamit spoke out against these injustices, going so far as to appear on a local
radio station. He was hunted down and in April 1980 was killed for his principled
stand regarding community land. Years later people still talk of his death as one in-
dicator that the violence of that era was moving closer and closer to the center of
Tecpán. That episode also has resonances with events of 1999, when huge forest
fires claimed some fourteen *caballerías* (or over 1,500 acres) in the forested mountains to the southwest of the town. Rumors circulated that the fires had been set to

cover up recent, illegal lumbering; people worried about the animals and trees lost; rural homes were threatened; children in town had nightmares about the fire invading their homes; and one man spoke of a dream at this sad, scary moment in which "*nuestros antepasados*" (our [Maya] ancestors) appeared before him expressing their hopes that the *costumbres* of the past would flourish again in daily life.

While the danger and unpredictability of rural areas is a prominent theme (and here we haven't even mentioned what the vagaries of weather mean to people whose lives depend on agriculture), another dominant sentiment expressed by Tecpanecos is the tranquillity of rural spaces and the beauty of the land. As the center of Tecpán grows more crowded and noisy, people wax poetic about the quiet and the green of *Madre Naturaleza* (Mother Nature). This might be linked to a general global awareness of environmental issues, but it also certainly relates to centuries-old Maya attachments to the earth as well as contemporary understandings of that affective history. (We discuss these cultural ties below.) However, in some eyes, numbers of Maya have moved—both literally and figuratively—far enough away from an intimate association with the land that concerted efforts must be made to preserve relatively untouched pieces and make these available to people seeking enjoyment, education, or reconnection. Thus, for example, immediately adjacent to the Iximche' archaeological park is the recently inaugurated *Jardín Botánico Maya "Jotay"* (The "Rebirth" Maya Botanical Park), the goals of which include the reawakening of people's awareness of nature and the preservation of a significant piece of pine and oak forest from the ax and hoe.

Along with these views of rural lands as both dangerous and bucolically pastoral, one could argue that farmers, at least, see land in straightforward material terms, as a productive resource. For some this is the primary, almost exclusive, value of land, but the majority of Kaqchikel farmers have strong affective ties to their lands as well, which are linked to heritage, social position, and social identity. What Sol Tax noted in his 1953 study of Panajachel largely holds true for Tecpán today: "to buy [land] increases and to sell it decreases not only wealth but prestige" and "in general, Indians appear to be loathe to sell their land, and sell it only when they deem it absolutely necessary"(1953: 68–69). Granted, there is a fair amount of land passing hands in Tecpán in a given year, and land prices in the late 1990s regularly surpassed the average in many parts of the United States ($1,500/*cuerda,* or approximately $5,220/acre). And yet land is in many ways unique as it resists complete commodification.

Land is more than an investment, more than an asset, as it is commonly viewed in the U.S. economy. Instead it represents a particular relationship between people and place, an intimate knowledge that even an increasingly hyper-mobile Guatemalan society has not erased. Land has histories attached to it, in particular, histories of ownership and relationships and knowledge passed from generation to generation. When talking to Tecpaneco farmers about their land one is likely to hear a several-generation history of its usage and passage from hand to hand. Land thus acts in part as a symbolic medium through which individuals connect with

Commodities

For objects to be considered "commodities" there must be some sort of fundamental similarity between them. Virtually everything that is mass produced is a commodity—cars, toilet paper, televisions—whereas original art is by nature the opposite of a commodity, each piece being unique. The economic value of commodification (beyond the economies of scale) is that, within certain categories at least, products may be bought sight unseen, giving rise to global commodities markets. In Volume I of his opus *Capital*, Karl Marx describes commodities as a by-product of capitalist production. He argues that commodification came about through the replacement of use-value (the practical use to which something will be put as embedded in a social network) with exchange-value (in which the value of an item is reduced to monetary terms, resulting in depersonalized relations between producers and consumers). The commodification of products was central to the emergence of long-distance trade and global markets. And late twentieth-century capitalism is marked by the rise of all sorts of new commodities (virtual dot com corporations, intellectual property, brand names, even black market human organs). Yet some products are immune to commodification because of their intrinsic individuality and relationship to the producer. For most farmers in Tecpán, land falls into this category. This is not to say that land is guarded at all costs simply for the sake of tradition; individuals and families do buy and sell land. But entering into the equation are the affective links, not just strictly economic cost-benefit analyses.

their ancestors, carrying on the traditions their families have practiced for generations. This is reinforced by a strong ethic of having children work the family land, and boys are sometimes actively discouraged from going to school or moving to another community so that they may continue to farm certain plots.

We have heard more than a few stories of individuals having to sell family lands, only to buy them back later. As one man explained, "selling our land is difficult, it hurts us to part with what our mothers and fathers gave us." Marcos and Maria are an elderly couple who have lived their entire lives in Tecpán on lands passed down through their families from as far back as anyone can remember. Marcos' father farmed *milpa* and occasionally planted some wheat, and Marcos grew up working the land and going to school. He married young and was given part of his father's land, which he worked to support his new family. Marcos and Maria eventually had one son and two daughters, and in the mid–1960s he began to work as an extension agent for a rural health care program. Through this work Marcos became convinced of the pressing need to spread modern health care to Guatemala's rural poor, and his three children grew up likewise fascinated with medicine. They all continued their studies through the local offerings in Tecpán and then went away to boarding schools to complete their educations. The two daughters became nurses and the son became a doctor. By the mid–1970s it seemed that none of Marcos' children would remain in Tecpán; his two daughters had married and moved to their husbands' towns and the son, who was studying medicine in the capital, said that that was where he wanted to live and practice. And so, with the Guatemalan economy worsening, Marcos sold a large part of the family lands in Tecpán. In the 1980s, however, one daughter, Marta, moved back to Tecpán with her husband, Juan, and their family. (Juan, a grade school teacher, had been assigned to a school in one of the *aldeas* of Tecpán.) Upon moving back to Tecpán, Juan and Marta lived with Marta's parents, saving up to buy a place of their own. And eventually they did, buying back some of the land that Marta's father had sold, land that they now hold dear, not just because of its productive capacity but because of the affective ties that it embodies.

Other families have other histories that relate to the tradition of lands coming into, moving out of, or remaining in family control. Some people, for example, bemoan the fact that family land was sold in generations past—sometimes, it is sadly noted, for foolish or rash reasons and at bargain prices—for which there is no hope of retrieval. A number of stories revolve around the inheritance of land by women, something that does not happen in every family or, if it does, might see the better land going to the sons and the poorer lands to the daughters ("because the daughters aren't likely to farm the land themselves"). The splitting of lands among offspring and the joining of lands in marriage also make for a genre of family accounts. For instance, when Eufemia and Juan married she brought a small but valuable piece of land into the union (it is located very close to the *cabecera*). Juan, however, was raised by his mother alone after his father died and raised very poor, so he entered the marriage landless. He worked several years to buy a piece of land some two kilometers outside of town. While Eufemia's land was divided up among the three children after her death, Juan continues to work his plot, which he knows in minute detail after working it for over forty years. Stories such as this repeat themselves today, with poorer men from *aldeas* marrying women from the *cabecera* and settling there, then working to raise money to buy a *milpa* plot within walking distance of town.

For Tecpán middle-class families that own land but cannot or for various reasons do not work it, owning the land is still important. Elderly couples, school teachers, municipal government bureaucrats, shop owners, and Tecpanecos working in Guatemala City all frequently maintain family plots in the *aldeas*. Commonly they enter into contractual agreements with a full-time farmer or another family member to work the lands. This arrangement customarily calls for the owner to supply land, seed, and fertilizer, and the farmer to work the land.

Often the harvest is split evenly between them, but there are also more straight monetary agreements of cash for work done. When someone other than the owners does the majority of the work on a plot, the male landowner might still insist on participating in some aspects of the growing cycle, not only to save money but also to participate in a central cultural tradition of Maya men. There is concern about whether Tecpán men and boys are upholding this tradition enough. People make comparisons with Patzún, for example, where (as one woman put it) "even doctors and lawyers go out on the weekends and work their land. You just don't find that as much here in Tecpán." This woman and her husband (a professional who does work their land some weekends) are trying to instill in their son the same love of and dedication to the land found in his grandfather (a farmer his whole life) and his father. The road to this appreciation is a bit bumpy, as the son groans about the prospect of a Saturday in the *milpa* weeding and digging while his younger brothers and sisters make plans to play soccer and watch TV after their morning chores.

To most Tecpán farmers, the attachment to their plots resides in the land's particularity, not in any abstract ideal of *milpa* agriculture. But from their attachment to the land, one may extrapolate a culturally conditioned desire to control one's means of production. The vast majority of farmers we have talked to believe that it is better to work as a farmer than as an employee. And their reasons all revolve around a common theme of controlling one's own means of production and destiny: "One is a slave working as an employee," "one wants his own land," "it is better to produce one's own necessities," "[in agriculture] one can decide when and how to work," and the most common response, simply that in farming "it is one's own" (*es propio*). Even people who aren't full-time farmers see the benefit in having some land under cultivation: If a family member were to lose a job, they would still have corn for the family or could sell any excess corn for additional income.

Rural Maya are often called peasants, or *campesinos* in Spanish, presumably because they are mostly impoverished farmers. The term "peasant," however, has become problematic in anthropological literature over the last few years. Classic definitions of peasantry stress that peasants provide almost all of their own subsistence needs, while having to offer surplus production as tribute. The problem with definitions of peasants, as with many such social categories, is that they promote a trait list approach to dividing up populations. What peasants do is rarely as clear cut as many definitions might have us believe. In practice there are a great many forms of adaptation to particular circumstances, and, in modern times at least, there are no classic peasants. This observation has led Michael Kearney (1996) to promote the term "post-peasants." Post-peasant households maintain strong ties to the land, growing at least a portion of their own food needs, while also engaging in other economic activities outside the domestic sphere. This engagement with larger economic systems often takes the form of occasional wage labor (very common among poor Tecpán households) and seasonal or semipermanent migration (to coastal plantations, to the capital, or even to the United States). Through the work of their

Figure 7.4   Land beside the Pan–American Highway, which runs along the right of this photograph, is preferred for growing broccoli and other nontraditional crops.

individual members, households are able to combine various economic strategies (subsistence agriculture, cottage industry, wage labor, etc.) to hedge their investments and ensure maximum security for the family unit as a whole.

FROM BEANS TO BROCCOLI AND MORE

To see the contemporary state of Maya agriculture one need only travel along the narrow two-lane stretch of the Pan-American Highway in Guatemala between Chimaltenango and Tecpán. Here lands once covered in corn, wheat, cabbage, and potatoes as recently as fifteen or twenty years ago now form a patchwork of broccoli, snow peas, and other nontraditional export crops (See Figure 7.4.).

Lori Ann Thrupp (1995) lists the characteristics of nontraditional agro-exports, which are increasingly important in developing economies around the world: high prices, highly perishable (requiring special handling and transportation and capital-intensive packing plants), monoculture (growing just one crop rather than rotating plantings), dependence on imported technology (notably, pesticides, herbicides, fertilizers, and hybrid seeds), and high quality control (buyers demanding uniformity of appearance).

The cold damp climate in the highlands around Tecpán (over 7,000 feet) is well suited to snow peas, broccoli, brussels sprouts, strawberries, raspberries, carnations, and other exotic produce. Guatemala has been able to play on a growing demand for such delicate and labor intensive crops and supply the U.S. market with rapidly increasing quantities of vegetables and berries. Of course exporting agricultural products is nothing new in Guatemala, where cochineal, indigo, coffee, cardamom, and cotton all have had long histories of large-scale production for the world market, but these new nontraditional exports favor smallholding Maya farmers in Tecpán in several important ways.

Beginning in the mid–1970s, USAID funded several programs to encourage nontraditional agricultural production in the Kaqchikel area. These included loan guarantees and public-private partnerships that sought to promote economic development while building on local agricultural expertise. Alimentos Congelados S.A. (ALCOSA), the first big exporter in the area, initially set up large plantations of cauliflower, snow peas, and broccoli. These proved inefficient because of high labor costs: Such exotic hybrid crops require frequent weeding, applications of pesticides and fertilizers, and generally close attention. So ALCOSA began to contract out crop production to smallholding farmers and several cooperatives. Their much-copied small-contract model has proved more efficient, providing packers with high-quality, low-cost products while significantly enriching a sector of petty agricultural capitalists who happen to be mostly Indians. This growth, however, has not been without costs. Small-scale producers who expanded into nontraditional production had a competitive advantage over plantations in that they could tap under-utilized reserves of unpaid household labor (especially of women and children). While this ideally results in an influx of cash to the household, it also sometimes pressures farmers to discourage their children from attending school and their wives from pursuing their own artisan production (of textiles, for example) and petty commerce, which may have detrimental long-term costs.

In some ways production of nontraditional agricultural exports is similar to *maquiladora* (offshore assembly) production. Hybrid seeds and seedlings, pesticides, fertilizers, and even packaging are largely imported from the United States; value is added through land use and local labor; and the products are exported, either fresh or frozen, benefiting from liberal U.S. tariff provisions. A crucial difference, and one that is highly valued in Maya culture, is that nontraditional producers retain control over their means of production, with the exception of carnations, which are most efficiently produced on plantations. Thus, by and large, nontraditional agricultural production is highly convergent with established local cultural and economic relations.

Nontraditional food crops grown around Tecpán have much shorter growing cycles than the *milpa*. Snow peas mature in as little as sixty days, and broccoli may be harvested after ninety days. This allows a fast turnaround that is very important to farmers, many of whom are constantly strapped for cash. But nontraditional production entails greater risks as well: larger investments and a greater percentage of crop failures. Nontraditional production has made some farmers wealthy, and these have been able to buy more land and hire workers to help them during harvest and planting. Others have lost their lands, having to sell to

Figure 7.5   Intermediaries buying broccoli in a hamlet of Tecpán.

the more successful export producers, and large expanses of land have been removed from subsistence *milpa* production.

Nontraditional produce is generally sold to either an intermediary or one of several packing plants and export companies in the area. Packing plants, several of which are subsidiaries of multinational corporations such as Dole, either pack the produce fresh, or, more commonly, flash freeze it so that, for example, peas and broccoli spears can be exported frozen. A packing plant not far from Tecpán is one of the largest flash-freezing facilities in the hemisphere, with a capacity of 50,000 kilograms per year. Smaller producers often sell to an intermediary (a *transportista*, or, more despairingly, a *coyote*), who offers lower prices but pays on the spot when produce is picked up (whereas packing plants often withhold full payment for up to several months) (See Figure 7.5). The market for nontraditional export crops in Guatemala matured rapidly in the late 1990s. With more and more farmers switching to nontraditional agricultural export crops, what was once a seller's market has become a buyer's market, allowing packing plants and *coyotes* to keep down the prices paid and resulting in some small farm failures.

As mentioned previously, the sole agricultural product that remains largely under the control of a corporate operation are carnations. On the outskirts of Tecpán, just alongside the Pan-American Highway, there are a number of tightly clustered football-field-sized greenhouses inside of which are tens of thousands of carnation plants, their flowers destined ultimately for florists in the United States (see Figure 7.6). The carnations are cut either late at night or very early in the morning, after which they are packed and trucked to Guatemala City's international airport for early morning flights, most going to Miami to clear customs. With this careful planning, most are in the United States within twenty-four hours ready to be shipped to regional floral distributors and then directly to flower shops across the country. When everything goes smoothly, they may be in homes in Des Moines or Seattle seventy-two hours after they are cut in Tecpán.

The carnation operation, owned and managed by a Guatemalan corporation, employs some 500 workers, making it the area's largest single local employer. Marta works on the carnation plantation, and her situation is not atypical of fellow employees. Marta is a widow and has two children, a girl and a boy ages thirteen and eight. The daughter works as a maid in neighboring households; the son

Broccoli

B roccoli is a relatively recent addition to the list of foods once considered luxuries and now seen as staples in U.S. diets. Broccoli consumption in the United States has increased more than 900 percent over the last twenty years, and the average American household now consumes some twelve pounds of broccoli annually.

A close relative of cauliflower and cabbage (also known as cole), broccoli is native to southern Europe, and was first grown commercially in the United States in the early 1920s. By 1925 iced broccoli was being shipped in large quantities from California to the urban markets of Chicago and New York. Broccoli is also known for thriving in cold, damp climates— just the sort of weather Tecpán has nearly year-round. Today, the United States produces some 1.5 billion pounds of broccoli a year, most in California but increasingly in Arizona, Florida, and Pennsylvania. The United States also imports large quantities of both fresh and frozen broccoli. Guatemala is one of its principal suppliers, exporting over 60 million pounds per year. This is a tiny percentage of the enormous U.S. market, but it is big pickings for Guatemala.

Figure 7.6   Greenhouses for growing carnations, which are shipped fresh to the United States and Europe.

is still in school; and Marta works at the carnation factory, where she made about Q600 a month (roughly $86) in 1994. She describes with animation the twenty-five flower beds for which she is exclusively responsible; she says that she misses them when she takes a vacation, that they are like children to her. Although the majority of the workers are Indian, Marta is a *ladina;* her husband was a Kaqchikel man. Neither of their parents fully accepted the marriage, and she feels very isolated in Tecpán, which was her husband's natal community. She is Protestant and seems to get a lot of comfort from going to the church. In addition, the carnation production allows her to continue to feel that she maintains control over her means of production, because of the exclusive care of the beds under her control.

The carnation plantation (or factory, perhaps, would be a more apt term) is a perfect example of "enclave development." It imports its seeds and fertilizer from and exports its product directly to the United States. It has established none of the sorts of local linkages that could stimulate grassroots development (buying seeds and seedlings locally, for example, which would encourage entrepreneurs to open greenhouses). And not all employees are as fond of their work as Marta; there is grumbling about low wages, long hours, and the foreign managers. At the same time, a different line of evidence suggests that working on the carnation plantation is seen as preferable to certain other employment alternatives. In 1999 and 2000, as the carnation plantation was expanding rapidly, household help was at a premium. It is the norm in all but the very poorest households in Tecpán to employ a domestic servant, usually a young woman or girl (the family's *muchacha*), who often lives with the family and works long hours for extremely low wages. But people complain that girls today no longer want to work as household servants, preferring the regular hours, ability to live at home, and relatively generous wages of the carnation plantation.

The effects of nontraditional agricultural production have included a dramatic redistribution of land, wealth, and the sorts of work some people do. In the case of food-producing lands, Tecpán plots have largely been transferred from the demographic minority (but economically more powerful) *ladino* population to Indians. At the same time, a nonlocal, non-Indian corporation has amassed huge tracts of land for non-food (i.e., carnation) production. What is more, nontraditional agriculture has created a greater local demand for wage labor, allowing men who formerly went to work during harvest on coastal sugarcane plantations to stay at home and work for larger nontraditional producers, or women who once would have worked as maids to find employment working with flowers. Laborers say that they prefer to work for these employers (even, in some cases, for slightly lower wages) to avoid the financial, emotional, and/or health costs associated with traveling away from their home communities. Finally, the presence of these new crops has had an impact on market sales and local consumption. Food products and flowers are sorted by grades, the lowest grades finding their way into the local market. When broccoli, for example, first appeared for sale in Tecpán, women didn't know what to do with it. It still remains something of a peripheral item in family meals, but it does make the occasional appearance.

JUANA AND PACO

Juana has a large permanent stall in the enclosed area of the Tecpán municipal market. The building is a drab cinder block construction, the whitewashed walls tinted a reddish-brown from the dust stirred up in the surrounding streets. Juana sits in the middle of four tables arranged in a square, sometimes barely visible over the mounds of fruit and vegetables, the bright colors of her *huipil* blending in with the produce. Her children play at her feet, and customers come and go, some visiting for a few minutes, others making their purchases and rapidly moving on to finish their day's shopping. Her husband Paco buys the produce in the capital and hauls it back to Tecpán. They use the money from her market earnings to finance their farming.

It is a cool and overcast July morning in the highlands of Guatemala, a couple of kilometers outside of town. It is the middle of the rainy season, and dark clouds promise an afternoon shower. Paco is working in his fields, land that has been in his family for generations. Today is a harvest day and, as Paco surveys the fields and organizes his brothers and hired helpers, Juana retires to the small thatch hut to begin lunch preparations. This is a scene played out countless times over the centuries throughout the Maya region—but Paco is not harvesting the corn, beans, and squash cultivated by his ancestors but rather broccoli and snow peas.

Paco is typical of a new generation of Maya farmers shifting their production away from traditional *milpas* to nontraditional export crops. He still grows *milpa*, but those plots are located on poorer land in a distant *aldea*; he reserves his best land for the lucrative export crops. In all, Paco and his brothers jointly own 20 *cuerdas* of land that they plant with nontraditional crops; Paco's portion is 7 *cuerdas*, and he rents one additional *cuerda* from a neighbor. He explains that the land that he owns was worked by his father, and his grandfather before that, and that he would never sell it.

Paco grows snow peas, cabbage, brussels sprouts, carrots, broccoli, beets, and radishes. He has been planting export crops, starting with broccoli, for fifteen years. He uses both organic and chemical fertilizers as well as chemical pesticides. The chemical fertilizers make for a good harvest, but they quickly exhaust the soil; thus organic fertilizer is used to replenish the nutrients. He also rotates the crops to replenish the soil. There is a twenty-four-hour waiting period after fumigation before crops can be harvested. The chemicals are very strong, and he uses gloves, boots, and a face mask when mixing and applying them; he says that neighbors have sometimes been careless and have become poisoned from applying chemicals. He has attended a number of courses sponsored by chemical, seed, and export companies, but he still admits he often does not fully understand the suggested application regimes.

Broccoli matures in about three months, and the harvest lasts for about two weeks as farmers comb through the fields cutting just ripened stalks three or more times a week. Paco harvests between 35 and 50 *quintales* per *cuerda* (or 1,200 to 1,700 pounds per acre). In a good harvest he earns between Q2,500 and Q3,000 (between $400 and $500 U.S. at 1994 exchange rates) per *cuerda* of broccoli, with expenses of Q600–1,000 for pesticide, seeds, fertilizer, and rent, leaving a Q1,500–2,400 profit (between $250 and $400). Paco was doing very well in 1993 and 1994, talking of buying new lands and hiring more employees. By 1999, however, he had suffered several crop failures and had pressing family health problems that required a lot of money, so he sold his land to one of his brothers and is working odd jobs around town.

Many other small-scale farmers who once grew broccoli and other nontraditional crops are now reverting those lands back to *milpa* because of the increasing financial risks, competition from more and more farmers, and concerns over pesticide use.

DISCUSSION

Given the opportunity, the majority of Tecpanecos choose to pursue economic strategies that allow them to maintain some degree of control over lands that produce at least part of their subsistence needs and that allow them to approximate the flexibility of labor inputs built into the agricultural cycle. A concern with control over means of production is not merely a form of resistance against capitalist incorporation (few, if any, Tecpanecos we know are ideologically op-posed to capitalism—and indeed they embrace it as a natural means of self-bet-terment) but also the maintenance of culturally valued relations of production. The rise of nontraditional agriculture in the Tecpán area is a case study in the convergence of macro-economic and local cultural and ecological factors. It shows how certain Maya farmers, based on cultural biases and available re-sources, have engaged, and in doing so helped define, the contours of global processes in this corner of the world.

Notes
1. In Tecpán and other rural Guatemalan communities, land is most often measured in *cuerdas*, a unit whose size varies from region to region. The Tecpán *cuerda* is equal to forty square *varas*, with a *vara* measuring roughly one meter (although individual farmers report different *vara* equivalencies, ranging from thirty-three to thirty-seven inches). Six Tecpán *cuerdas* make up a *manzana*, which equals 0.7 hectares. Thus, there are 8.6 Tecpaneco *cuerdas* to a hectare, and a hectare equals 2.471 acres.

Further Reading
Goldin, Liliana R. 1996. Economic mobility strategies among Guatemalan peasants: Prospects and limits of nontraditional vegetable cash crops. *Human Organization* 55(1): 99–107.

Kearney, Michael. 1996. *Reconceptualizing the peasantry: Anthropology in global perspective.* Boulder, CO: Westview Press.

Tax, Sol. 1953. *Penny capitalism: A Guatemalan Indian economy.* Smithsonian Institution Institute of Social Anthropology Publication No. 16. Washington, DC: Smithsonian Institution.

Watanabe, John M. 1992. *Maya saints and souls in a changing world.* Austin: University of Texas Press.

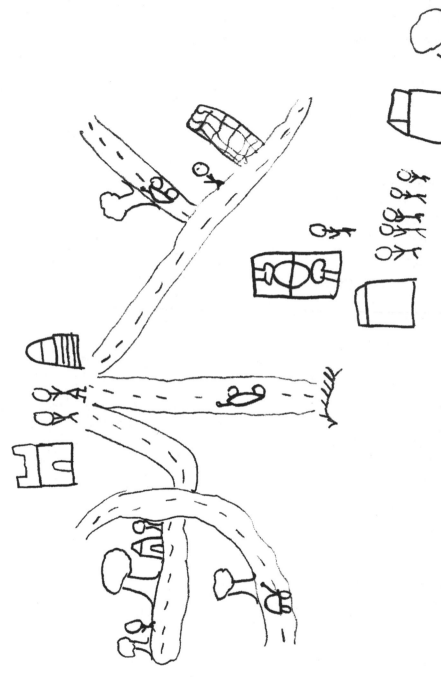

The roads of Tecpán, drawn by Juan Alberto Patal Ajzac (age 6).

Conclusion:
Tecpán Maya in the
Contemporary World

Along with their deep historical roots, the Maya have long been known for their extensive routes. The *sakb'e* ("white ways," the raised roads made of stone) of the Classic Maya linked cities, fostered trade, and marked the authority of the urban center whose ruler was strong enough to order them built. Today's roads also tell stories of the Maya towns transected and connected by them (see Adams 2001).

Stand on a street in Tecpán and you get a series of snapshots of the very public activities that go on in the municipality and that link it to the larger twenty-first-century world. You hear the sounds of pigs and carts, motorcycles and drunks, firecrackers and lovers. You smell the stink of diesel fuel, the resinous sweetness of *pom* (incense), and the aroma of firewood burning and tortillas toasting on the other side of walls. You see signs for Sony and Pepsi, a doctor trained in Israel, a marimba orchestra, a pizza parlor, and a Kaqchikel cooperative hardware store. And you watch people passing: a woman heading to the neighborhood mill to get corn ground into *masa*, children returning "Rugrats" to the video rental shop, and two men carrying a long pole between them from which hang dozens of skeins of rayon threads made in Mexico, dyed in Tecpán, and ready to be sold in neighboring communities.

Roads are regarded as potentially dangerous. They are the nighttime lairs of men who turn into monkeys, soldiers, and gang members (or at least spray-paint-toting teenagers) who write "BREAKERS" and "SALVATRUCHAS" on walls. Unsupervised children on the streets run the risk of being hit by speeding cars or falling into the wrong crowd. Neighbors may steal neighbors' animals that stray out onto the street. And during the *violencia*, barbed wire "tacks" strewn on

145

the Pan-American Highway posed a danger for vehicles while dead bodies lining the highway at regular intervals warned, "This too could be you."

But roads also offer the town a sense of *communitas*. Processions fill the streets for Corpus Christi and Semana Santa. Loudspeakers from churches and chapels blare Bible passages at passersby. The enormous Thursday market consumes more and more road space each year—reaching out now to include pickup trucks piled high with *ropa usada*, the flotsam of more affluent lives in *los Estados Unidos*—and thousands of people jam the streets and plazas to buy and sell. Other crowds of people in the roadways mark hours, days, and months on the calendar: school children coming and going to classes; buses arriving and departing from the capital; farmers walking to their fields with seed and, months later, returning to their homes with their harvest; tourists—foreign and national—headed out for a day at Iximche'; and trucks passing through with U.S. wheat for the mill (and this in a town known from colonial days until very recently for its homegrown grain) and broccoli destined for foreign markets. Government officials still have their say about roads, and local and national politics get played out in cinder blocks and asphalt. After years of crying "wolf," the government paved the road to Iximche' and the long-promised inauguration was held; before that a woman whose house lies on this more and more busy street commented that Tecpán had seen more promises of pavement than actual work.

Part of the great shift in academic conversation that started at the end of the twentieth century involves a rethinking of the relationship between local and global processes, a recognition that things are often not as bounded as they might seem, that communities "leak." This means that the ideas and "objects" that hold them (whether the latter are material or not) are carried into and out of communities via roads, footpaths, radio waves, telephone wires, and more; that the "local" is constantly challenged by the "foreign" and shifting and being redefined or restated because of this. Embedded in the notion of "leakage" is the idea of "process," that social life must be understood by focusing on practice. From this perspective, meaning is not static; it emerges, shifts, is interpreted, and gets reconfirmed through the actions of individuals or groups engaged in public behavior. Putting these two ideas together, community life must be understood in terms of ongoing processes that may involve elements from a number of spheres.

In anthropology the ideas about boundedness and community have been played out in part by what makes it into the ethnographic narrative. Whereas in the past it was all too common for an anthropologist to go into a community blinkered and focused only on the "native" population and their "traditional customs," ethnographers now regularly include "Westerners," the "colonial representatives," and themselves in their presentations. As for "traditional customs," whereas fieldworkers of the past attempted "salvage anthropology"—again with a particular kind of focus and framing—which preserved the oldest and most authentic traditions before they disappeared forever, anthropologists today are more willing to admit that what they (and perhaps the people they worked with) understood as "traditional" was a development within the past fifty to one hundred years and perhaps now only practiced by a few elders who, in their youth, probably were not "traditional" at all. This is not to deny the existence of what people call "traditional" or the deep genealogies of behaviors and objects, but rather to recognize the ongoing nature of life and the shaping of meaning.

We have used these ideas and a range of theoretical works to inform our narrative account of life in Tecpán. Our experiences in the community have shown us both the profound sense of history carried (like the work of the ancient *cargadores* or daybearers) by the place as well as some of the surprising (to us, at least) juxtapositions enabled by the flow of information, goods, and people into and out of Tecpán in recent years. Thus, while some of our chapters might seem like the "usual" categories of ethnographies of the past and our focus on Maya Indians a popular one, we would argue that we have aimed to consider this oft-examined group through the lens of their actions in and knowledge of a whole range of social spheres in this (post)modern world. The result, we hope, is a portrait other than the "exotic Maya" of travelogues and New Age guides or the "peasant Maya" of Third World narratives or the Maya as "anonymous victims/guerrillas" of newspaper commentaries during Guatemala's civil war. Rather, our desire is that indigenous Tecpanecos emerge as more "real," a group of people struggling to make ends meet but also struggling to make sense of their ethnic heritage, the sometimes shifting/sometimes unmovable forces of life, and the ways of a complex and multi-perspectival world.

To that end we want to close with a snapshot of some multi-generational concerns, our conversation starting around a dining room table. This could be almost any night and a scene in many Tecpán homes, at least one with an anthropologist listening in. This particular table conversation takes a sudden turn when the five-year-old announces that when he grows up he's going to be an evangelical pastor first and then a *soldado* (the latter meaning "soldier," but in this case perhaps not referring to a member of the Guatemalan military but to the toy "cowboys and Indians"—called *soldados*—that he plays with each day). His older brothers and sisters snicker at this pronouncement and go on to offer their "more reasonable" choices. "Me, a doctor," one of the other brothers pronounces. "And me, a lawyer," the oldest child, a daughter about to enter her teens, adds. The mother, a teacher, comments on her children's ambitions and that they'll have to go to Guatemala City to study for those careers, if the family can afford them at all. Meanwhile her father, a farmer his entire life, sits quietly listening; her husband is absent because his government job several hours away from home means he can't commute.

On other occasions the mother has talked about how much her children have to learn about the "reality" of being *indígena* in a *ladino*-dominant world. One daughter, she says, is already suffering from prejudicial treatment at school by a teacher who is anti-Indian and playing favorites with the *ladino* students in the class. The mother has been trying to inform her children about the different sorts of discrimination they will face and how they might handle those situations. For example, once on a day trip to Guatemala City the mother and her oldest son went to eat at a Pizza Hut. The waitress ignored them and the mother eventually flagged down the manager and, in the middle of the restaurant and in front of other (*ladino*) customers, told him that it wasn't good business for his staff to discriminate against Indians. The son was mortified and just wanted his mother to stop, but his mother said, "He has to learn. Some day he'll be there by himself and he needs to learn to defend himself."

And so a new generation of Kaqchikeles make their place in the world—instructed by their parents, constrained by power structures out of their immediate control and motivated by their own hybrid desires for the future. What it means to be an Indian in Tecpán is rapidly changing, refracted through personal histories that are themselves permeated with connections to local society, national structures, and global cultural flows. Out of this diversity of responses and initiatives arise constantly morphing patterns, redefining and reorienting the discursive community of Tecpaneco Kaqchikeles in an ever-emergent future.

Glossary

Aj itz—A religious specialist associated with malevolent sorcery, a "witch"; see also *Brujería*

Aj q'ij—"Day-keeper," a benevolent religious specialist or spiritual guide

Alcalde—"Mayor," also the highest office in a *cofradía*

Aldea—"Village," a small community that is tied politically to a municipal center; see also *Cabecera* and *Municipio*

Anima—A vitalistic force unique to humans, located in the heart (from the Spanish *ánima*, "spirit")

Backstrap loom—A hand loom used for weaving the *po't*, is anchored to a tree or a pole and stretched taut by a strap that goes around the back of the weaver

Brujería—"Witchcraft," used as a derogative reference to traditional Maya religion

Cabecera—"Town center," the seat of municipal government

Caserío—"Hamlet," an administrative and rural territorial unit that is part of a *municipio*, smaller than an *aldea*

Cholq'ij—Kaqchikel term for the Maya Calendar Round

Cofradía—Catholic religious brotherhoods introduced by the Spaniards but today considered characteristically Maya

Colegio—A private primary and/or secondary school

Compadrazgo—Godparenthood

Corte—See *Uq*

Costumbre—"Customs," commonly used to denote more traditional elements of Maya culture

Cuerda—A measurement of land that varies between communities in Guatemala; in Tecpán it is equivalent to 0.11 hectares

Evangélico—A member of a Protestant sect, most of whom practice "evangelical" Christianity

Finca—A large farm, often including a number of household compounds and owned by an absentee landlord

Huipil—See *Po't*

Indigenismo—A modernist social and political philosophy that emerged in Latin America in the late nineteenth century and promoted the cultural assimilation of Indians

INGUAT—The Instituto Guatemalteco de Turismo, the Guatemalan tourist promotion board

Kaxlan—Non-Maya or foreign, from Maya derivations of "castellano" or "Spanish"

K'iche'—The ethno-linguistic group that borders Kaqchikel territory to the northwest

K'u'x—Variously translated as "heart," "soul," "center," or "essence"

Ladino—A non-Indian Guatemalan, generally considered to be of mixed blood descent and socialized in Spanish and Western-based culture. Most *ladinos* in Guatemala do not use the term to describe themselves, although it is frequently employed by scholars and Maya.

Masa—The moist corn dough used to make tortillas and tamales

Mestizo/a—A person of "mixed" blood, a term of self-identification preferred by some *ladinos*

Metate—A grinding stone

Milpa—Plots of primarily maize and beans, usually inter-planted with various types of squash; considered to be the traditional basis of Maya subsistence

Monte—Uninhabited forests and mountainsides outside town

Muchacha—"Girl," a household servant

Municipio—"Township," an important administrative unit below the level of regional departments in Guatemala; often considered to be the primary referent of Indian self-identity

Nervios—"Nerves," a common ailment

Pedida—Ritualized marriage request

Pila—An outdoor sink with a deep holding tank for water and surfaces on which clothes and dishes are washed. *Pilas* are found in most households in Tecpán, and the town also maintains a number of communal *pilas*.

Pom—A type of incense used in Maya ceremonies made from tree resin

Po't—A blouse woven in a traditional Maya style with designs associated with particular Maya communities; *huipil* in Spanish

Pueblo—Usually translated as either "people" or "town" depending on the context. In pan-Mayanist discourse it has come to be associated with more inclusive notions of community.

Quetzal—The Guatemalan unit of currency. In 1981 the currency was on par with the dollar; in 2001 the exchange rate was up to 7.9 quetzales to the U.S. dollar.

Quintal—A weight of 100 pounds

Rij po't—A handwoven over-blouse worn on ceremonial occasions

Rodillera—An apron-like piece of apparel woven from wool and worn as part of the traditional Kaqchikel male dress

Sobrehuipil—See *Rij po't*

Susto—"Fright," a potentially deadly ailment in which part of the soul leaves the body following a sudden fright

Tuj—A traditional Maya sweatbath used for both bathing and ritual purposes

Traje—Traditional Maya dress, for women consisting of a *po't* and an *uq*, considered to be a primary emblem of ethnic identity for Maya women

Troje—A room or small separate building in household compounds where dried maize is stored

Uq—A wraparound skirt worn as part of traditional Maya women's traje; *corte* in Spanish

URNG—The Unidad Revolucionaria Nacional Guatemalteca or Guatemalan National Revolutionary Front

USAID—The United States Agency for International Development

Vestido—"Clothing," specifically Western-style clothing as opposed to *traje*

(la) Violencia—The period of violence from the late 1970s through the mid–1980s in Guatemala

Winäq—A Maya person; also "twenty"

Xajan—Taboo, forbidden

References

Adams, Abigail E. 2001. The transformation of the *tzuultaq'a*: Jorge Unico, Protestants and other Verapaz Maya at the crossroads of community, state, and transnational interests. *The Journal of Latin American Anthropology* 6(2): 198–233.

Appadurai, Arjun. 1996. *Modernity at large: Cultural dimensions of globalization.* Minneapolis: University of Minnesota Press.

Asturias, Miguel Angel. 1964 [1946]. *El señor presidente.* Translated from the Spanish by Frances Partridge. New York: Atheneum.

Borg, Barbara E. 1980. Iximché: The last great struggle for New World supremacy. Unpublished manuscript in the archives of the Centro de Investigaciones Regionales de Mesoamérica (Antigua Guatemala).

Bricker, Victoria R. n.d. Linguistic continuities and discontinuities in the Maya area. In *Between the past and the future: Maya culture, history, and identity in postcolonial Mexico and Guatemala*, edited by John Watanabe and Edward F. Fischer. Santa Fe, NM: School of American Research Press.

_____. 1981. *The Indian Christ, the Indian king: The historical substrate of Maya myth and ritual.* Austin: University of Texas Press.

_____. 1973. *Ritual humor in highland Chiapas.* Austin: University of Texas Press.

Carlsen, Robert S. 1997. *The war for the heart and soul of a highland Maya town.* Austin: University of Texas Press.

Carmack, Robert. 1981. *The Quiché Mayas of Utatlán: The evolution of a highland Guatemala kingdom.* Norman: University of Oklahoma Press.

Carmack, Robert M., ed. 1988. *Harvest of violence: The Maya Indians and the Guatemalan crisis.* Norman: University of Oklahoma Press.

Casaús Arzú, Marta Elena. 1992. *Guatemala: Linaje y racismo.* San José, Costa Rica: FLACSO.

Chayanov, A. V. 1966 [1925]. *The theory of peasant economy.* Homewood, IL: American Economic Association.

Clifford, James. 1988. *The predicament of culture: Twentieth-century ethnography, literature, and art.* Cambridge, MA: Harvard University Press.

Coe, Michael D. 1992. *Breaking the Maya code.* New York: Thames and Hudson.

Coe, Sophie D. 1994. *America's first cuisines.* Austin: University of Texas Press.

Cojtí Cuxil, Demetrio. 1997. *Ri maya' moloj pa Iximulew; El movimiento maya (en Guatemala).* Guatemala City: Editorial Cholsamaj.

_____. 1994. *Políticas para la reivindicación de los Mayas de hoy (fundamento de los derechos específicos del Pueblo Maya)*. Guatemala City: Cholsamaj.

_____. 1991. *Configuración del pensamiento político del Pueblo Maya*. Quetzaltenango, Guatemala: Asociación de Escritores Mayances de Guatemala.

_____. 1990. Lingüística e idiomas Mayas en Guatemala. In *Lecturas sobre la lingüística maya*, edited by Nora England and Stephen R. Elliot, pp. 1–25. Antigua, Guatemala: Centro de Investigaciones Regionales de Mesoamérica.

_____. 1984. Problemas de la identidad nacional guatemalteca. *Revista Cultura de Guatemala* V(1): 17–21.

De Janvry, Alain. 1981. *The agrarian question and reformism in Latin America*. Baltimore, MD: The Johns Hopkins University Press.

Demarest, Arthur. 2003. *Ancient Maya: The rise and fall of a rainforest civilization*. Cambridge: Cambridge University Press.

Duranti, Alessandro, ed. 2001. *Key terms in language and culture*. Malden, MA: Blackwell Publishers.

Editorial Cholsamaj. 1996. *Runa'oj ri K'amöl B'ey Seattle/La Carta del Jefe Seattle*. Guatemala City: Editorial Cholsamaj.

Ehlers, Tracy Bachrach. 1990. *Silent looms: Women and production in a Guatemalan town*. Boulder, CO: Westview Press.

Eley, Geoff. 1994. Nations, publics, and political cultures: Placing Habermas in the nineteenth century. In *Culture/power/history: A reader in contemporary social theory*, edited by Nicholas B. Dirks, Geoff Eley, and Serry B. Ortner, pp. 297–335. Princeton, NJ: Princeton University Press.

England, Nora. 1996. The role of language standardization in revitalization. In *Maya cultural activism in Guatemala*, edited by Edward F. Fischer and R. McKenna Brown, pp.178–194. Austin: University of Texas Press.

Escobar, Arturo. 1995. *Encountering development: The making and unmaking of the Third World*. Princeton, NJ: Princeton University Press.

Falla, Ricardo. 1994. *Massacre in the jungle*. Boulder, CO: Westview.

Farriss, Nancy M. 1984. *Maya society under colonial rule: The collective enterprise of survival*. Princeton, NJ: Princeton University Press.

Fischer, Edward F. 2001. *Cultural logics and global economies: Maya identity in thought and practice*. Austin: University of Texas Press.

_____. 1999. Cultural logic and Maya identity: Rethinking constructivism and essentialism. *Current Anthropology* 43(4): 473–499.

Fischer, Edward F., and R. McKenna Brown, eds. 1996. *Maya cultural activism in Guatemala*. Austin: University of Texas Press.

Foster, George. 1967. *Tzintzuntzan: Mexican peasants in a changing world*. Boston: Little, Brown.

_____. 1965. Peasant society and the image of the limited good. *American Anthropologist* 67(2):293–315.

Fox, John W. 1978. *Quiché conquest: Centralism and regionalism in highland Guatemalan state development*. Albuquerque: University of New Mexico Press.

Freidel, David. A., Linda Schele, and Joy Parker. 1993. *Maya cosmos: Three thousand years on the shaman's path.* New York: William Morrow.

Gálvez Borrell, Víctor, and Alberto Esquit Choy. 1997. *The Mayan movement today: Issues of indigenous culture and development in Guatemala.* Guatemala City: FLACSO.

Garrard-Burnett, Virginia. 1998. *Protestantism in Guatemala: Living in the new Jerusalem.* Austin: University of Texas Press.

Garzon, Susan, R. McKenna Brown, Julia Becker Richards, and Wuqu' Ajpub' (Arnulfo Simón). 1998. *The life of our language: Kaqchikel Maya maintenance, shift, and revitalization.* Austin: University of Texas Press.

Goldin, Liliana R. 1996. Economic mobility strategies among Guatemalan peasants: Prospects and limits of nontraditional vegetable cash crops. *Human Organization* 55(1): 99–107.

Goldman, Francisco. 1992. *The long night of the white chickens.* Boston: Atlantic Monthly Press.

Goody, Jack. 1982. *Cooking, cuisine, and class.* Cambridge: Cambridge University Press.

Gossen, Gary H. 1999. *Telling Maya tales: Tzotzil identities in modern Mexico.* New York: Routledge.

———. 1974. *Chamulas in the world of the sun: Time and space in a Maya oral tradition.* Cambridge, MA: Harvard University Press.

Green, Linda. 1999. *Fear as a way of life: Mayan widows in rural Guatemala.* New York: Columbia University Press.

Gudeman, Stephen, and Alberto Rivera. 1990. *Conversations in Colombia: The domestic economy of life and text.* Cambridge: Cambridge University Press.

Gupta, Akhil, and James Ferguson. 1992. Beyond "culture": Space, identity, and the politics of difference. *Cultural Anthropology* 7(1): 6–23.

Handler, Richard, and Eric Gable. 1997. *The new history in an old museum: Creating the past at colonial Williamsburg.* Durham, NC: Duke University Press.

Handy, Jim. 1984. *Gift of the devil: A history of Guatemala.* Toronto: Between the Lines.

Hendrickson, Carol. 1995. *Weaving identities: Construction of dress and self in a highland Guatemala town.* Austin: University of Texas Press.

———. 1991. Images of the Indian in Guatemala: The role of indigenous dress in Indian and Ladino constructions. In *Nation-states and Indians in Latin America,* edited by Greg Urban and Joel Sherzer, pp. 287–306. Austin: University of Texas Press.

Heptig, Vince. 1997. *A Mayan struggle: Portrait of a Guatemalan people in danger.* Fort Worth, TX: MayaMedia Publishing.

Hill, Robert M. 1992. *Colonial Cakchiquels: Highland Maya adaptations to Spanish rule, 1600–1700.* Fort Worth, TX: Harcourt Brace Jovanovich.

———. 1989. Social organization by decree in colonial highland Guatemala. *Ethnohistory* 36(2): 170–198.

Hill, Robert M., and Edward F. Fischer. 1999. States of heart: An ethnohistorical approach to Kaqchikel-Maya ethnopsychology. *Ancient Mesoamerica* 10: 317–332.

Instituto Guatemalteco de Turismo. 1992. *Guatemala: Colorful and friendly.* Guatemala City: Instituto Guatemalteco de Turismo.

Jonas, Susanne. 1999. *Of centaurs and doves: Guatemala's peace process*. Boulder, CO: Westview Press.

_____. 1991. *The battle for Guatemala: Rebels, death squads, and U.S. power*. Latin American Perspectives Series, No. 5. Boulder, CO: Westview Press.

Kearney, Michael. 1996. *Reconceptualizing the peasantry: Anthropology in global perspective*. Boulder, CO: Westview Press.

Kirshenblatt-Gimblett, Barbara. 1998. *Destination culture: Tourism, museums, and heritage*. Berkeley: University of California Press.

Kleinman, Arthur. 1988. *The illness narratives: Suffering, healing, and the human condition*. New York: Basic Books.

Lakoff, George, and Mark Johnson. 1980. *Metaphors we live by*. Chicago: University of Chicago Press.

Laughlin, Robert. 1975. *The great Tzotzil dictionary of San Lorenzo Zinacantán*. Washington, D.C.: Smithsonian Institution.

Lovell, W. George. 1992. Heavy shadows and black night: Disease and depopulation in colonial Spanish America. *Annals of the Association of American Geographers* 82(3): 426–443.

Lovell, W. George, and Noble David Cook, eds. 1991. *Secret judgments of God: Old World disease in colonial Spanish America*. Norman: University of Oklahoma Press.

Lutz, Christopher H., and W. George Lovell. 1990. Core and periphery in Colonial Guatemala. In *Guatemalan Indians and the state, 1540 to 1988*, edited by Carol A. Smith, pp. 35–51. Austin: University of Texas Press.

Mallon, Florencia E. 1994. The promise and dilemma of subaltern studies: Perspectives from Latin American history. *American Historical Review* 99: 1491–1515.

Manz, Beatriz. *1988. Refugees of a hidden war: The aftermath of counterinsurgency in Guatemala*. Albany: State University of New York Press.

Marcus, George E., and Michael M. J. Fischer. 1986. *Anthropology as cultural critique: An experimental moment in the human sciences*. Chicago: University of Chicago Press.

Menchú, Rigoberta. 1984. *I, Rigoberta Menchú, An Indian woman in Guatemala*. Edited and translated by Elisabeth Burgos-Debray. London: Verso.

Moberg, Mark. 1992. *Citrus, strategy, and class: The politics of development in southern Belize*. Iowa City: University of Iowa Press.

Monaghan, John. 1995. *The covenants with earth and rain: Exchange, sacrifice, and revelation in Mixtec sociality*. Norman: University of Oklahoma Press.

Montejo, Victor. 1987. *Testimony: Death of a Guatemalan village*. Willimantic, CT: Curbstone Press.

Nash, June C. 1970. *In the eyes of the ancestors: Belief and behavior in a Maya community*. New Haven: Yale University Press.

Nelson, Diane M. 1999. *A finger in the wound: Body politics in quincentennial Guatemala*. Berkeley: University of California Press.

Otzoy, Irma. 1996. Maya clothing and identity. In *Maya cultural activism in Guatemala*, editied by Edward F. Fischer and R. McKenna Brown, pp. 141–155. Austin: University of Texas Press.

Oxlajuuj Keej Maya' Ajtz'iib'. 1993. *Maya' chii': Los idiomas Mayas de Guatemala.* Guatemala City: Editorial Cholsamaj.

Pakal B'alam [José Obispo Rodríguez Gurján]. 1994. *Kojtz'ib'an pa Kaqchi'/Leamos y Escribamos Kaqchikel.* Guatemala City: Editorial Cholsamaj.

Paul, Benjamin D., and William J. Demarest. 1988. The operation of a death squad in San Pedro La Laguna. In *Harvest of violence: The Maya Indians and the Guatemalan crisis,* edited by Robert M. Carmack, pp. 119–154. Norman: University of Oklahoma Press.

Raxche'(Demetrio Rodríguez Guaján). 1996. Maya culture and the politics of development. In *Maya cultural activism in Guatemala,* edited by Edward F. Fischer and R. McKenna Brown, pp. 74–88. Austin: University of Texas Press.

————. 1992. Introducción. In *Cultura maya y políticas de desarrollo,* 2d ed. Chimaltenango, Guatemala: COCADI.

Richards, Michael. 1985. Cosmopolitan world-view and counterinsurgency in Guatemala. *Anthropological Quarterly* 3:90–107.

Sahlins, Marshall. 1974. *Stone age economics.* Chicago: Aldine.

Sam Colop, Enrique. 1996. The discourse of concealment and 1992. In *Maya cultural activism in Guatemala,* edited by Edward F. Fischer and R. McKenna Brown, pp. 107–113. Austin: University of Texas Press.

Saq'be Editorial. 1997. *Nuk'ulem chi rij kib'anikil chuqa' kich'ojib'al ri Achamaq'i'/Acuerdo sobre indentidad y derechos de los Pueblos Indígenas.* Chimaltenango, Guatemala: Editorial Saqb'e and Editorial Cholsamaj.

Schele, Linda, and David Freidel. 1992. *A forest of kings: The untold story of the ancient Maya.* New York: Quill/William Morrow.

Schele, Linda, and Mary Ellen Miller. 1986. *The blood of kings: Dynasty and ritual in Maya art.* Fort Worth, TX: Kimbell Art Museum

Scheper-Hughes, Nancy. 1992. *Death without weeping: The violence of everyday life in Brazil.* Berkeley: University of California Press.

Schirmer, Jennifer. G. 1998. *The Guatemalan military project: A violence called democracy.* Philadelphia: University of Pennsylvania Press.

Scott, James C. 1990. *Domination and the arts of resistance: Hidden transcripts.* New Haven, CT: Yale University Press.

————. 1985. *Weapons of the weak: Everyday forms of peasant resistance.* New Haven, CT: Yale University Press.

Simon, Jean Marie. 1987. *Guatemala: Eternal spring, eternal tyranny.* New York: W. W. Norton.

Smith, Carol A. 1991. Maya nationalism. *NACLA Report on the Americas* 23(3):29–33.

————. 1990. Introduction: Social relations in Guatemala over time and space. In *Guatemalan Indians and the state, 1542–1988,* edited by Carol A. Smith, pp.1–30. Austin: University of Texas Press.

Smith, Waldemar. 1977. *The fiesta system and economic change.* New York: Columbia University Press.

Stoll, David. 1999. *Rigoberta Menchú and the story of all poor Guatemalans.* Boulder, CO: Westview Press.

_____. 1990. *Is Latin America turning Protestant?: The politics of evangelical growth.* Berkeley: University of California Press.

Stonich, Susan. 1993. *"I am destroying the land!": The political ecology of poverty and environmental destruction in Honduras.* Boulder, CO: Westview Press.

Tax, Sol. 1953. *Penny capitalism: A Guatemalan Indian economy.* Smithsonian Institution Institute of Social Anthropology Publication No. 16. Washington, DC: Smithsonian Institution.

_____. 1937. The municipios of the midwestern highlands of Guatemala. *American Anthropologist* 39(3): 423–444.

Tedlock, Barbara. 1982. *Time and the highland Maya.* Albuquerque: University of New Mexico Press.

Tedlock, Dennis. 1985. *Popol Vuh: The definitive edition of the Mayan book of the dawn of life and the glories of gods and kings.* New York: Touchstone.

Thrupp, Lori Ann. 1995. *Bittersweet harvests for global supermarkets: Challenges in Latin America's agricultural export boom.* Washington, DC: World Resources Institute.

Turner, Victor. 1969. *The ritual process: Structure and anti-structure.* Chicago: Aldine.

UNDP (United Nations Development Programme). 2000. *Human development report 1999.* Oxford: Oxford University Press.

UNDP-Guatemala. 1999. *Guatemala: El rostro rural del desarrollo humano.* Guatemala City: UNDP-Guatemala.

Van den Berghe, Pierre L. 1981. *The ethnic phenomenon.* New York: Elsevier.

Warren, Kay B. 1998. *Indigenous movements and their critics: Pan-Maya activism in Guatemala.* Princeton, NJ: Princeton University Press.

_____. 1993. Interpreting *la violencia* in Guatemala: Shapes of Kaqchikel silence and resistance in the 1970s and 1980s. In *The violence within: Cultural and political opposition in divided nations,* edited by Kay B. Warren, pp. 25–56. Boulder, CO: Westview Press.

_____. 1978. *The symbolism of subordination: Indian identity in a Guatemalan town.* Austin: University of Texas Press.

Watanabe, John M. 1992. *Maya saints and souls in a changing world.* Austin: University of Texas Press.

Whorf, Benjamin Lee. 1941. The relation of habitual thought and behavior to language." In *Language, thought, and reality: Selected writings of Benjamin Lee Whorf,* edited by J. B. Carroll. Cambridge, MA: MIT Press.

Wierzbicka, Anna. 1997. *Understanding cultures through their key words: English, Russian, Polish, German, and Japanese.* New York: Oxford University Press.

Wolf, Eric R. 1986. The vicissitudes of the closed corporate community. *American Ethnologist* 13: 325–329.

_____. 1957. Closed corporate peasant communities in Mesoamerica and Central Java. *Southwestern Journal of Anthropology* 13(1): 1–18.

Index